GUARDIANS OF LIBERTY

GUARDIANS OF LIBERTY

BY LINDA BARRETT OSBORNE

FREEDOM OF THE PRESS AND THE NATURE OF NEWS

ABRAMS BOOKS FOR YOUNG READERS

NEW YORK

*For Lily and her generation, that they
may grow up in a country that values honesty
and freedom of expression*

Title page: American eagle and coat of arms. Woodblock. 1882.
Incidental line illustrations: Introduction: Gavel. Chapter 1: Inkwell and goose feather quill pen. Chapter 2: Early printing press. Chapter 3: Linotype typesetting machine. Chapter 4: Vintage radios. Chapter 5: Vintage television. Chapter 6: Notepad, pen and press pass. Chapter 7: Space satellite. Chapter 8: Mobile phone. Microphone. Chapter 9: Megaphone.

Cataloging-in-Publication Data has been applied for and may be obtained
from the Library of Congress.

ISBN 978-1-4197-3689-6

Text copyright © 2020 Linda Barrett Osborne
Edited by Howard W. Reeves
Book design by Erich Lazar

Printed and bound in U.S.A.
10 9 8 7 6 5 4 3 2 1

Abrams Books for Young Readers are available at special discounts when purchased
in quantity for premiums and promotions as well as fundraising or
educational use. Special editions can also be created to specification. For details,
contact specialsales@abramsbooks.com or the address below.

Abrams® is a registered trademark of Harry N. Abrams, Inc.

ABRAMS The Art of Books
195 Broadway, New York, NY 10007
abramsbooks.com

CONTENTS

INTRODUCTION

C ongress shall make no law . . . abridging the freedom . . . of the press," states the First Amendment to the United States Constitution. This amendment was one of ten—called the Bill of Rights—added to the Constitution in 1791. For more than 220 years, it has guaranteed that the federal government cannot stop news media from publishing news, ideas, and opinions, even those that disagree with the actions and policies of presidents and lawmakers. Protecting any American's printed news or opinion is exactly what the First Amendment was meant to do.

We live in a time when media technology—the way news is delivered—has changed dramatically. It is also a time when much of the news has been attacked by a president as being fake and unbelievable. Knowing the story of why freedom of the press was important to the Founding Fathers—men like Benjamin Franklin, Thomas Jefferson, and James Madison—and how it has stayed a strong principle in American law and culture can help us understand its value today.

This engraving shows portraits of four of the Founding Fathers. George Washington is at the top, and the others are (left to right) Thomas Jefferson, James Madison, and John Adams. The founders of the United States believed that freedom of the press was an essential right.

There were government complaints about the press and calls to censor it even before the United States became a country. There was also a feisty, very partisan press. A partisan is someone who supports one political party's point of view and not the other. It is true of much of the media today. It is striking how similar the issues have been over the last two hundred years. Basic questions about freedom of the press have not changed. How does the press act as a watchdog against government abuses? Can freedom of the press exist in time of war without endangering national security? Why does it matter that different points of view are represented? From the beginning of our country, Americans have debated these questions—often in the press itself.

They have also been debated in Supreme Court hearings and decisions. This book explores the way that the Supreme Court has helped interpret the meaning of freedom of the press over time. Challenges to total press freedom usually come through the courts, and their decisions are used to shape the decisions in newer cases. The controversial areas where the law sets limits to press freedom are national security, discrediting another person (libel), offending community values (this includes pornography), and incitement to violence based on hatred of a group because of race, politics, religion, or gender. Another question Americans ask is, are these limits valid or should there be no limits at all?

Often, the press reports information or opinions that we would rather not know or consider. Accepting ideas that we agree with is easy. Accepting the publication of ideas we dislike, fear, or believe damage our country or some of its people—or that are negative about ourselves—is much harder. "The principle of free thought—not free thought for those who agree with us but freedom for the thought that we hate"—is an important principle of the Constitution, wrote famous Supreme Court Justice Oliver Wendell Holmes Jr. in 1929. That is the heart of press freedom: that everyone, even if we disagree strongly with them, has a right to be heard.

When the Founding Fathers came to create the Bill of Rights, they included freedom of the press because they believed that a democracy needs an active, vital press representing all points of view. They thought that the best way to preserve democracy was to encourage debate based on reading different accounts and opinions. Open discussion of ideas and their faults or merits would eventually lead to the best solutions for everyone. A free press would encourage Americans to think, argue, and defend all ideas. "Freedom of speech is a principal pillar of a free government," wrote Benjamin Franklin. "When this support is taken away, the constitution of a free society is dissolved."

The Founding Fathers also believed in a press that would be a watchdog over government. These were men who had rebelled against their rulers during the American Revolution because they believed the British government, led by the king and Parliament, was unfair. They wanted a press that would point out and criticize bad decisions rather than say only good things about leaders and lawmakers. One way to protect the people from government interference was to let them know when their political leaders were acting badly.

"There is nothing so *fretting* and *vexatious*; nothing so justly TERRIBLE to tyrants . . . as a FREE PRESS," wrote Samuel Adams in the *Boston Gazette* eight years before the Revolution. "The reason is obvious; namely, Because it is . . . '*the bulwark of the People's Liberties*.'" (A bulwark is a barrier built to defend against danger.) In 1778, poet, playwright, and essayist Mercy Otis

The Battle of Lexington was one of the first clashes with British soldiers during the American Revolution. Before and during the war, much of the American press was active in supporting both press freedom and the move for independence.

Warren wrote of the dangers of a government without a free press. The rulers, while gaining power, might "suffer men to think, say or write what they please; but when once established . . . the most unjust restrictions may take place . . . And an *imprimator* [permission necessary to publish] on the Press . . . may silence the complaints, and forbid the most decent remonstrances of an injured and oppressed people."

A free press, not controlled by the government, could gather information; it could expose decisions and policies that were unfair to the American people. It could let people know about things the government did not want them to know.

George Washington is shown here in full military dress in a portrait by Rembrandt Peale. Washington was the first president of the United States and the first to receive negative press.

The person the Founding Fathers most feared could abuse his or her power—and who needed to be watched closely—was the president. At the Constitutional Convention in 1787, the delegates hotly debated whether the country should have a president at all, and if so, how much power he should have. Charles Pinckney, a delegate from South Carolina, expressed the dilemma. He wanted a "vigorous Executive," but not one that could totally control "peace & war," which, he believed, "would render the Executive a monarchy, of the worst kind, to wit an elective one." In other words, even an elected president might assume the absolute powers of a king. In the end, the convention decided the United States should have one elected president, limited in his or her power by Congress and the Supreme Court. They also counted on a free press to keep an eye on the president.

Because the way Americans feel about presidents and their politics varies widely, no president can count on only "good" press. So from the early days of our country, the amendment guarding press freedom put the president—regardless of his political party—and the press at odds with each other. If the news printed about the president was favorable, he liked the press. If it was negative or disapproving, he didn't. Most presidents have objected to news that does not agree with them or shows them in a bad light.

This was the situation when the United States was founded and it is the same today. Combative, hurtful words about presidents are not new in our history. John Adams, Thomas

Jefferson, Andrew Jackson, Abraham Lincoln, Woodrow Wilson, Richard Nixon, George W. Bush, Barack Obama, and Donald Trump are among the presidents who have been ripped apart in the news.

Even George Washington, the first president and the "father of our country," got bad press. Benjamin Franklin Bache, who took over his grandfather Benjamin Franklin's press, charged that Washington had encouraged "political iniquity and . . . legalized corruption" during his presidency. Washington was "possessed of power to multiply evils upon the United States," Bache wrote in the Philadelphia *Aurora*.

"Every president will try to use the press to his best advantage and to avoid those situations that aren't to his advantage," President Ronald Reagan (1981–1989) said in a 1988 speech.

Ronald Reagan, fortieth U.S. president, enters a room full of reporters for a press conference.

"The press can take care of itself quite nicely, and a president should be able to take care of himself as well." Reagan was talking about a give-and-take, where each side has strength and the press and the president each have their own roles. His words were in keeping with the First Amendment.

The Founding Fathers did not call for freedom of the "news." They talked about freedom of the press. What they meant by "the press" was very different from what we think of now. The word came from the fact that, from the fifteenth century on in Europe, news was printed on a machine that "pressed" the ink into the paper. Today's way of printing is usually digital and all done by computer-controlled machines. Eighteenth-century presses were operated by one person at a time, letter by letter and by hand.

In the eighteenth century, "press" meant only newspapers, pamphlets, and broadsides—single poster-like sheets of paper—put out by a few independent printers. Now the technology for reaching people has changed dramatically. We draw our news from media that did not exist then: television, radio, film, video, and the internet, where anyone can reach an audience as fast as she or he can tap "enter" on a smartphone or computer. News travels more rapidly than it once did and comes from many hundreds of sources. When writing about the last one hundred years, it is more accurate to say "news media" than simply the "press" or "newspapers."

What makes up "the news"? It is both the factual reporting of events and the expression of opinions. These include editorial

EARLY PRINTING TECHNOLOGY

In the mid-fifteenth century, Johannes Gutenberg of Germany invented a way to print paper using letters cast in molten metal spooned into molds. Gutenberg wasn't the first to discover printing. In China, letters were cast in clay as early as the eleventh century. In Europe, people used woodblocks to print pictures. What was special about Gutenberg's invention was that the cast letters could be moved to form words and sentences in different parts of the text. This method was called "movable type." It was all done by hand and was time-consuming, but faster than anything that had come before for printing multiple copies of the same page. Others made improvements to the press, but this basic method was still being used in the 1700s.

This printing press belonged to Founding Father Benjamin Franklin. It is typical of the presses used in the eighteenth century.

opinions that come from the editors and lead writers of a media source and represent their views. They also include letters to the editor and articles expressing opinions, often written by experts on a topic, who may not be regular contributors to a news source. Media also offer entertainment, but entertainment is not news. Sometimes, though, entertainment indirectly comments on important current events. Late-night television shows, from *Saturday Night Live,* which premiered in 1975, to Samantha Bee on TBS, have done this using comedy.

Like all people, all news media have points of view, and their opinions of events can differ widely. Many express the beliefs of political parties—Republican, Democratic, or other groups, like the Green Party, which focuses on protection of the environment, or the Socialist Party, which believes government, not private individuals, should control basic services like health insurance and utilities. Even in the straight reporting of events, news media must decide which stories and events to highlight. They also must decide which to ignore. If they don't report a story or event, it will not reach those Americans who rely on that source for information. Americans today overwhelmingly tend to follow the news whose point of view they already agree with, whether in newspapers (print or online), blogs, radio, or television. But the Founding Fathers wanted more debate of different opinions, not less or none at all.

The Founding Fathers also knew that what the press publishes can be false—sometimes deliberately, sometimes by mistake. Opinion can be confused with fact. But facts can be proved to be true or false. If the temperature is measured as ninety-five degrees in Phoenix, Arizona, that is a fact. One opinion about it may come from a person living in Phoenix, who thinks "That's not so hot. It's quite comfortable." A visitor from Minnesota might run to an air-conditioned room because the heat is "unbearable." Those are *opinions* about how hot it is. They don't change the *fact* that the temperature is ninety-five degrees.

Since Donald Trump was elected president in 2016, talk of "fake news" has been widespread. The "fake news" he complains

This photo at Barack Obama's first inauguration shows the crowds reaching from the Capitol Building (on the right) *to the Washington Monument. It was taken at 11:22 A.M. by the National Park Service on January 20, 2009.*

about is the news that is negative about him or his policies—the "thoughts that he hates," as Oliver Wendell Holmes Jr. would say. Just after the January 2017 inauguration of President Trump, he disagreed with news reports saying that the crowd at his ceremony was smaller than that at President Barack Obama's first inauguration. Photographs showed that Obama's crowd was clearly bigger. A presidential counselor to Trump explained that they were stating "alternative facts." An alternative is a different position to take on what is being considered. There are no alternative facts, only alternative opinions about them.

But President Trump is not wrong that the press has its biases. Americans who disagree with many of his policies think the media

The crowds at Donald Trump's inauguration on January 20, 2017, start at the Capitol building (back of photo, center) but reach only partway toward the Washington Monument. They are visibly smaller in this photograph than the crowds at Obama's inauguration eight years earlier. The photo was taken by the National Park Service at 11:53 A.M., thirty-one minutes after the time of the Obama inauguration photograph.

that supports Trump is incorrect or misinformed. This raises several questions. What responsibilities does the press have to investigate and present the news fairly? How has new technology had an impact on the press and on the way we receive information? Is democracy harmed when an entire set of opinions is dismissed without considering its value, or when factual news reporting is labeled false without proof? Is it harmed when the press is censored for expressing opinions the government does not like?

Perhaps there are no absolute answers to these questions. But in the spirit of discussion and debate encouraged by the First Amendment, we can consider the history of the facts and opinions before us. We can come to our own conclusions about how to keep democracy strong in the United States.

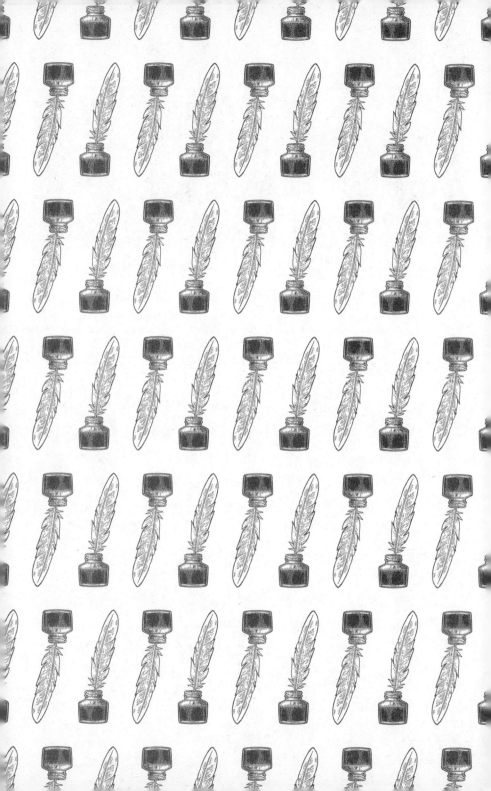

CHAPTER 1

THE EIGHTEENTH CENTURY:
PARTISAN PRESS AND REVOLUTION

John Peter Zenger had been in jail for eight months when, on August 4, 1735, he was put on trial for printing harsh words about the British governor of New York. The United States did not exist then. The British king had appointed a royal governor to rule some of the colonies. In this case it was William Cosby, who was angry because Zenger's newspaper, the *New-York Weekly Journal*, had said he was greedy and selfish and that he denied people their liberties.

In 1735, New York and the other colonies followed English law. Although they had legislatures made up of colonial settlers, they thought of themselves as Englishmen and -women who happened to live far away from the mother country. For many years, nothing could be published in Britain without a government license; anything that was written could be censored by the government and would never appear in print. By the time of Zenger's trial, that had changed. There was no more government censorship in England that kept an article or opinion from being printed. But once it

Lawyer Andrew Hamilton defends printer John Peter Zenger at his trial in 1735.

was printed, the printer could be fined or sent to jail for saying negative things about the king, or the British Parliament, or any government official—for example, a colonial governor like Cosby.

The crime of publishing strong criticism of the government was called "seditious libel."

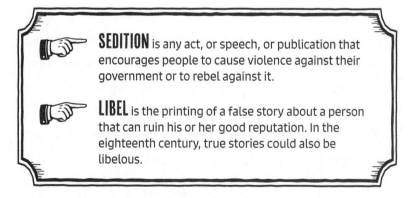

SEDITION is any act, or speech, or publication that encourages people to cause violence against their government or to rebel against it.

LIBEL is the printing of a false story about a person that can ruin his or her good reputation. In the eighteenth century, true stories could also be libelous.

★ **16** ★

Seditious libel was thought to put the security of the government—and therefore, the country—in danger. The tradition of English law said that it did not matter if what was printed was true or false. In fact, it was worse if the negative comments were true. No one needed to take false statements seriously. But true statements, if they were proved and accepted as true, gave the people even more reason to criticize their government and perhaps overthrow it. "If people shall not be called to account for possessing the people with an ill opinion of the government, no government can subsist," stated John Holt, a judge in England in 1704. "For it is very necessary for all governments that the people should have a good opinion of it." For Holt and English law, any writing that questioned the behavior of the government "has always been looked upon as a crime." Therefore, the author of something true could be punished with heavier fines and longer jail sentences than the author of something false.

Now came John Peter Zenger's case in 1735, heard before a court set up by Governor William Cosby. Zenger had printed the *New-York Weekly Journal*, but he did not write the words that bothered Cosby. Cosby could not know who had actually written the words. In colonial America, many authors used pen names different from their real names. Some used more than one pen name so that it would look like different people had expressed the same opinion. Readers might guess who the real authors were, but courts could not prove who actually wrote the articles. Instead, they brought the printer to trial. Zenger was a German immigrant who ran his press as a business, printing other people's work and not his own. Although Cosby had offered a reward of fifty pounds (today worth nearly $13,000) to anyone who could name the authors, no one identified them.

At the trial, New York's attorney general, Richard Bradley, represented the government. Bradley spoke to the twelve-man jury (women did not serve on juries at the time). He called

Andrew Hamilton successfully defended John Peter Zenger by asking the jury to consider whether truth was more important than falsehoods.

Zenger "a seditious person and a frequent printer and publisher of false news and seditious libels" who had "wickedly and maliciously" meant to do harm to Cosby's reputation. The jury's only job was to decide if Zenger had actually printed the articles. Judges would decide whether this was seditious libel and what the punishment should be.

The lawyer who represented Zenger, Andrew Hamilton—no relation to Alexander Hamilton—had come from Pennsylvania. He was known throughout the colonies for his legal skill. He astonished everyone in court by agreeing that Zenger was the printer. Attorney General Bradley then told the jurors that they had to find Zenger guilty and reminded them that under British law—their law—seditious libel was worse if what was printed was true rather than false.

Hamilton asked if the jury really believed that "truth is a greater sin than falsehood."

HE ARGUED:

It is natural, it is a privilege, I will go farther, it is a right, which all free men claim, that they are entitled to complain when they are hurt. They have a right publicly to ... [fight back] against the abuses of power in the strongest terms, to put their neighbors on their guard against the ... open violence of men in authority, and to assert with courage the sense they have of the blessings of liberty ... The question before the Court and you, Gentlemen of the jury, is not of small or private concern. It is not the cause of one poor printer, nor of New York alone, which you are now trying. No! It may ... affect every free man that lives under a British government on the main of America. It is the best cause. It is the cause of liberty.

The jury believed that Zenger had indeed printed the truth and, more important, that this was no crime. It returned a verdict of not guilty.

This broadside of the Declaration of Independence was the first
publication to feature the names of the signers. It was printed by
Mary Katherine Goddard. Goddard was one of more than a dozen
women who ran printing presses in colonial America.

Why did the Cosby government accept the decision and free Zenger? Perhaps the court and Cosby realized that public opinion was for Zenger. To go against it could well cause greater conflict. More and more, the colonists were discussing the meaning of freedom and their relationship to Britain. The outcome of the Zenger trial did not change the law of seditious libel. But after that, no printers—or authors—in America were charged in colonial courts for criticizing the royal government.

While Zenger was in jail, his wife, Anna, had taken over printing the *New-York Weekly Journal* until the trial was over. When John Peter died in 1746, Anna took over again and, unafraid, continued to criticize the British government. In the eighteenth century, women edited some sixteen out of a total of seventy-eight family-owned, weekly newspapers printed in the colonies. They included Elizabeth Timothy, Anne Catherine Hoof Green, Clementina Bird Rind, and Mary Katherine Goddard, who printed the first newspaper that carried the names of all but one of the signers of the Declaration of Independence. The signers had not wanted their names published when the Declaration was first made because they were basically committing treason against the British king. In 1777, Goddard was allowed to publish a broadside of the Declaration with their names. A line at the bottom read "Printed by Mary Katherine Goddard." Hers is the only woman's name printed on a copy of the Declaration of Independence.

In the years between the Zenger case and the Declaration of Independence in 1776, the number of newspapers in the

COLONIAL NEWSPAPERS

Newspapers in the colonies were different from what they are today. Usually they were one large page of paper, printed on the front and back. Later, some of them increased to four pages. The printer usually printed his or her stories right out of British newspapers, without changes, just as they appeared in the original. Colonists were eager to hear the news from England. Printers published the news from other colonies and from foreign papers as well.

To help make money, colonial newspapers also included essays, often on political and religious topics, that they were paid to publish. These expressed the opinions of everyone from government officials to ordinary citizens. They represented many different, often conflicting, perspectives. In fact, the same issue could include articles on the same event or subject that gave different facts and points of view. Newspapers also included advertisements. But by the late 1700s, printer and publisher Isaiah Thomas pointed out, "News do[es] not appear to be always the first object of editors." Instead, "gazettes and journals are now chiefly filled with political essays." Some printers chose not to publish the essays they disagreed with, while others printed anything they were paid to print.

colonies increased. The *Boston News-Letter*, founded in 1704, was the first newspaper to successfully print for several years—and the only newspaper until 1719, when the *Boston Gazette* began printing. By 1740—five years after Zenger's trial—sixteen weekly newspapers were published in the colonies. By 1775, the number had grown to thirty-seven.

In March 1765, the British Parliament passed a law that had a huge impact on printers. The Stamp Act called for a tax on paper used in the colonies to print everything from legal documents to land deeds to playing cards—and newspapers. Each piece of paper had to come from England, where it was officially stamped. Money from the tax would pay for thousands of soldiers to guard the

Bostonians burn copies of proclamations declaring the Stamp Act of 1765. Most colonial newspapers ignored or protested the tax on stamps, and the British Parliament later repealed the law.

boundary with colonies claimed by the French in America. Colonists did not want to pay for housing British soldiers; they did not believe they were in danger from French attacks. More important, Parliament passed the act with no say from the colonists who served in colonial legislatures. The colonists called it "taxation without representation."

Cadwallader Colden, the alarmed royal lieutenant governor of New York, sent a report to Britain about the terrible articles appearing in colonial newspapers. He said they were "filled with every falsehood that malice could invent to serve their purpose of exciting the People to disobedience of the Laws and to sedition." The newspapers were expressing what the colonists were feeling: anger at the royal government for not giving them a voice

★ 23 ★

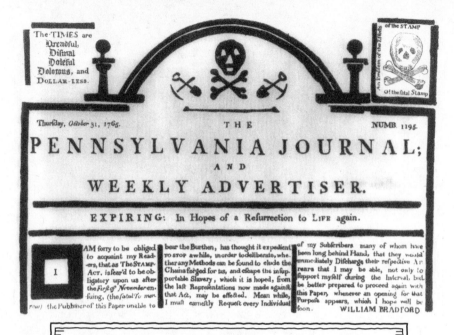

The TIMES are
Dreadful,
Dismal,
Doleful
Dolorous, and
DOLLAR-LESS.

of the STAMP

An Imblem of the Effects

Of the fatal Stamp.

Thursday, *October* 31, 1765. NUMB. 1195.

T H E

PENNSYLVANIA JOURNAL;

A N D

WEEKLY ADVERTISER.

EXPIRING: In Hopes of a Resurrection to LIFE again.

I AM sorry to be obliged to acquaint my Readers, that as The STAMP Act, is fear'd to be obligatory upon us after the *First of November* ensuing, (the *fatal To morrow*) the Publisher of this Paper unable to bear the Burthen, has thought it expedient TO STOP awhile, in order to deliberate, whether any Methods can be found to elude the Chains forged for us, and escape the insupportable Slavery, which it is hoped, from the last Representations now made against that Act, may be effected. Mean while, I must earnestly Request every Individual of my Subscribers many of whom have been long behind Hand, that they would immediately Discharge their respective Arrears that I may be able, not only to support myself during the Interval, but be better prepared to proceed again with this Paper, whenever an opening for that Purpose appears, which I hope will be soon. WILLIAM BRADFORD

The October 31, 1765, issue of the Pennsylvania Journal and Weekly Advertiser
*used thick, black lines of mourning and a skull and crossbones to emphasize how
the cost of the stamp tax would be the death of colonial newspapers.*

in making the laws that applied to them. A secret organization called the Sons of Liberty formed in 1765. The group opposed the Stamp Act, but its aims were bigger—to guarantee freedom in every way for the thirteen colonies.

The day before the Stamp Act went into effect, the *Pennsylvania Journal* printed thick black lines around its pages, as if mourning a person's death. Instead of a stamp, the newspaper printed a skull where the stamp should be. A coffin appeared on the last page, explaining how the paper had died because of an illness: "a STAMP in her Vital . . . [organs]." The *New-Hampshire Gazette* said of itself, "*I must Die*, or submit to that which is *worse* than Death, *be Stamped*, and lose my Freedom."

Several colonial newspapers defied the act after stamps were required. They continued to publish without them. Opposition from the colonies was so strong that Parliament repealed the Stamp Act one year later, in March 1766. This victory encouraged the colonial press. Printers realized that they could break the law and not be punished. Their power came from royal governors' fear that attacking the press might lead the public to attack them. A few printers were brought before colonial legislatures, but none were fined or sent to jail.

The press that opposed the Stamp Act supported the growing call for a break with Britain. These colonists came to be known as patriots (or Whigs, after the liberal British party). But there were those who wanted to remain a British colony. They were called loyalists (or Tories). After 1766, loyalists also printed newspapers that opposed the patriots and supported the British government.

Patriot publications increasingly supported liberty from Britain, and completely supported freedom of the press—their own press. Mobs of patriots attacked loyalist presses, destroying their machinery and attacking the printers themselves. Many loyalist printers fled the cities where they had lived. The patriot press reported that a mob "fired Bullets into the House" of one loyalist and "obliged him to fly from it to save his life." Another had his guns stolen and "one of his fine Horses poisoned." A third "was confined & bound for 36 Hours, & not suffered to lie in a Bed, & threatened to be sent to" an underground prison. Some loyalist printers were tarred and feathered—covered with hot wood tar, then with feathers that stuck to the tar—and paraded through

A Virginia mob forces a loyalist to sign a document that says he will not support Britain during the American Revolution. A sack of feathers and a barrel of hot tar await in the background if he does not pledge his allegiance to the patriots. These loyalty documents were published as broadsides.

the streets. For the most part, patriots did not live up to Oliver Wendell Holmes Jr.'s ideal of freedom of the press: to allow freedom for the thought you hate.

As the Revolutionary War progressed, more loyalist printers were forced out of business. In May 1775, "One Hundred Pounds Lawful Money Reward" was offered for the capture of printer Isaac Wilkins, who with a group of loyalists had written, "We are determined at the hazard of our lives and properties to support the King." Wilkins, however, fled to Canada, as many loyalists did. Other loyalists were forced to take back what they had said about loyalty to the British government. Their apologies were printed on broadsides and distributed.

Newspapers, pamphlets, and broadsides played a large part in uniting the colonies. After the war, Founding Father John Adams wrote: "The [thirteen] colonies had grown up under constitutions of government so different; there was so great a variety of religions; they were composed of so many different nations; their customs, manners, and habits had so little resemblance . . . that to unite them in the same . . . system of action was certainly a very difficult enterprise." But printed materials could go along with travelers from colony to colony or be sent through the colonial mail system. People in Massachusetts could read about what people in Virginia were thinking and doing. South Carolina could learn about New Hampshire. As long as the press remained free—and newspapers moved freely—information could help the colonies recognize that they all had the same goal: freedom from Britain.

The American Revolution ended in 1783. The colonies won their victory. They became the United States. Each new state wrote its own constitution about how it would be governed. By 1791, nine of the thirteen states had named freedom of the press as a right. "Freedom of the Press is one of the greatest bulwarks of liberty," stated the Virginia constitution in familiar words, "and can never be restrained but by despotic [tyrannical] Governments."

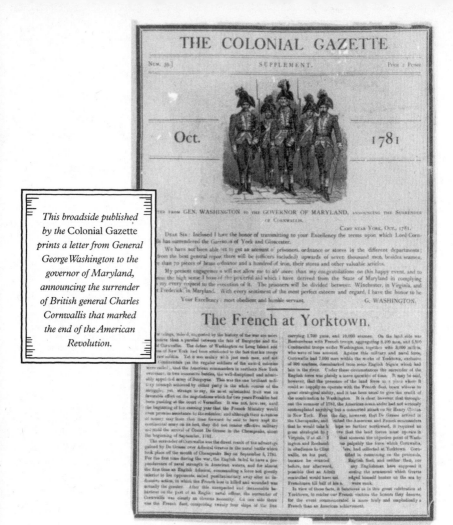

This broadside published by the Colonial Gazette *prints a letter from General George Washington to the governor of Maryland, announcing the surrender of British general Charles Cornwallis that marked the end of the American Revolution.*

Massachusetts's constitution declared, "The liberty of the press is essential to the security of freedom in a state: it ought not, therefore, to be restrained."

But the Constitution of the United States, approved by the majority of states in 1788, did not mention press freedom. It told how the government should be organized, but it did not state specific rights that the people should have. After more than two years of debate, the ten amendments known as the Bill of Rights were added in 1791. The First Amendment states:

"Congress shall make no law respecting an establishment of religion, or prohibiting the free exercise thereof; or abridging the freedom of speech, or of the press; or the right of the people peaceably to assemble, and to petition the government for a redress of grievances."

Freedom of the press was paired with "freedom of speech": speech for the spoken word, press for the printed word. Sometimes it is hard to draw the line between speech and press, but both are protected. They both come under the category "freedom of expression." The First Amendment applied only to federal laws made by Congress. Many states were able to pass laws against press freedom. These could only be challenged in federal courts after the Fourteenth Amendment, passed in 1868, gave all American citizens equal protection under the law.

How strong would the First Amendment be? Since 1791, presidents, lawmakers, courts, the military, journalists, and ordinary Americans have given different answers to that question.

CHAPTER 2

CONGRESS DOES MAKE A LAW . . .

It didn't take long for a president to be angered by the comments about him in newspapers. John Adams, who was the vice president of the United States under George Washington, was the second president in his own right, from 1797 to 1801. He was also the first president to tackle the press head-on for its negative comments against him and his administration. "There is nothing that the people dislike that they do not attack," Adams complained. "They attack officers of every rank in the militia and in the army, members of congress, and congress itself, whenever they dislike its conduct." The way they attacked the government was through the press.

The press had been partisan before the Revolution, taking the side of patriots or loyalists. The press in 1797 was strongly partisan, and the opinions newspapers expressed were even more insulting to those they opposed. Newspapers were divided into supporters of Adams and his Federalist political party and supporters of Thomas Jefferson, then called Republicans (but

This portrait of President John Adams, surrounded by the coats of arms of sixteen states, was printed and sold in 1799, the year after Congress passed the Sedition Act. By 1799, in addition to the original thirteen colonies, Kentucky, Tennessee, and Vermont had become states.

not connected to today's Republican Party), who was Adams's vice president.

Adams wanted a law that would officially make seditious libel of the new American government a crime.

His supporters in Congress argued that the law was needed to stop criticism of the government that could create dangerous discord. There were political tensions with France, and Americans sympathetic to France might upset the newly formed country. Adams and Congress maintained this was a question of national security. But Albert Gallatin, a congressman supporting

Jefferson, said that "this bill must be considered only a weapon used by a party in power in order to perpetuate their authority and preserve their present places." How would it be used? he asked. "Only by punishing persons of politics different from those of the administration." The bill passed anyway. It was signed into law by Adams on July 4, 1798.

Authors could be fined and/or jailed under the Sedition Act if found guilty of "any false, scandalous and malicious writing . . . against the government of the United States, or either house of Congress . . . or the President . . . with intent to defame . . . or to bring them . . . into contempt or disrepute; or to excite against them . . . the hatred of the good people of the United States." This was a return to the policies of royal colonial governments. Seditious libel had hardly existed as a crime in the United States until Congress, urged by Adams, brought it back again.

When Matthew Lyon, a Jefferson ally and congressman, published a letter in the *Vermont Journal* criticizing Adams for his "continual grasp of power, in an unbounded thirst for ridiculous pomp, foolish adulation and selfish avarice [love of ceremony, need to be admired, and greed]," he was convicted under the Sedition Act. He was fined $1,000 (a little over $20,000 in today's currency) and sentenced to four months in jail. Lyon was forced to stay in jail when he could not pay the fine. Jefferson supporters from around the country raised the money to pay it for him.

The issue of seditious libel versus freedom of the press was largely political. It was a duel between two parties that each saw the nature of the United States differently. Under the Sedition Act there was freedom of the press—but only for those newspapers that supported Federalists. The cases tried before the courts were those of authors who criticized the Adams government. The Sedition Law did not protect Adams's vice president, Thomas Jefferson, at all.

Supporters of Jefferson immediately attacked the law. Jefferson himself, and James Madison, main author of the Constitution and the Bill of Rights and a future president, persuaded lawmakers in Virginia and Kentucky to speak out. "The constitutional power

Vermont representative Matthew Lyon and Roger Griswold of Connecticut fight on the floor of Congress after the House of Representatives refused to expel Lyon for spitting tobacco at Griswold. The fight showed the tensions between those who supported John Adams's policies and those who supported the policies of Thomas Jefferson's party. Fistfights were rare but did occur.

exercised over the press by the 'sedition-act,' ought more than any other, to produce universal alarm," stated the *Virginia Report* of 1800, "because it is levelled against the right of freely examining public characters and measures, and of free communication among the people . . . which has ever been justly deemed the only effectual guardian of every other right."

For the presidential election of 1800, Jefferson ran against Adams. Neither candidate campaigned for himself, but supporters on each side used the press to attack the other. A pamphlet published by newspaper editor James Callender said that Adams was a "strange compound of ignorance and ferocity, of deceit and weakness" who "has neither the force and firmness of a man, nor the gentleness and sensibility of a woman." In 1800, Callender was found guilty of violating the Sedition Act with such writings. He paid a $200 fine (equivalent to a little more than $4,000 in today's currency) and spent nine months in jail.

Adams's supporters called Jefferson a "weakling," an "atheist," and a "coward." Still, Jefferson won the 1800 election for president. The Sedition Act expired with his election. It was set up by Adams's supporters to end when a Federalist was no longer in power so that Jefferson could not use the same act to censor his critics. Federalist newspapers continued to attack Jefferson for his policies.

Jefferson had often praised freedom of the press before this election campaign: "The basis of our governments being the opinion of the people, the very first object should be to keep

THE CALL
TO DUTY

JOIN
THE
ARMY

FOR HOME
AND COUNTRY

ADAPTED
FROM THE
SCULPTURE BY
EDOARDO
CAMMILLI

PUBLISHED BY RECRUITING COMMITTEE OF THE
MAYOR'S COMMITTEE ON NATIONAL DEFENCE

A poster calls for American men to enlist in the army when the United States entered World War I in 1917. Congress would soon pass laws requiring strict censorship of written materials during the war.

that right" he wrote in 1787, "and were it left to me to decide whether we should have a government without newspapers, or newspapers without a government, I should not hesitate a moment to prefer the latter." But twenty years later, in 1807, after years of being criticized in the press, Jefferson wrote to a friend: "Nothing can now be believed which is seen in a newspaper. Truth itself becomes suspicious by being put into that polluted vehicle. The real extent of this state of misinformation is known only to those who are in situations to confront facts within their knolege [knowledge] with the lies of the day." Jefferson was frustrated by negative press coverage, but he did not encourage passing a law that would punish it.

More than a hundred years would go by before Congress again passed laws abridging the freedom of the press. Again, the declared reason was to protect national security. When the United States entered World War I (1914–1918) in 1917, President Woodrow Wilson told Congress, "If there should be any disloyalty, it will be dealt with with a firm hand of stern repression."

In every war, governments on both sides count on the support of their citizens. They encourage patriotism and seek to silence those who speak out against any aspect of the war. Governments also make military and political policy decisions that need to be kept secret. If the enemy were to gain this information, the safety—the security—of the country would be in danger. This is what all presidents leading the United States during a war have believed. So have most members of Congress. With the country at war, it is easy to argue that some kind of censorship is necessary. World War I raised the question of what was more important: discouraging media opinions that might be sympathetic to the enemy, or protecting the First Amendment right?

Congress passed the Espionage Act in June 1917. It was the biggest challenge to freedom of the press since the Sedition Act of 1798 under John Adams. Although "espionage" usually means spying, this act stated, "Every letter, writing . . . postal card . . . photograph, newspaper, pamphlet, book, or other publication . . . of any kind, containing any matter advocating or urging treason, insurrection, or forcible resistance to any law of the United States, is hereby declared to be nonmailable." Under the act, patriotism and loyalty could be questioned, as well as the impact on national security.

The Democratic Party held the majority in Congress when the Espionage Act was passed. The press was not happy. "Why, Senators, the Democratic party originated in the OPPOSITION of Thomas Jefferson and James Madison to JUST EXACTLY SUCH LAWS AS THIS UNAMERICAN LAW," the *San Francisco Examiner* pointed out. Except for censoring information about "military and naval movements," wrote the *Examiner*, "there is no possible excuse for denying the American papers the fullest and most accurate news of what is occurring in the country and the World."

Even if there had been no Espionage Act, most newspapers during World War I voluntarily followed government "guidelines"

Albert Sidney Burleson was postmaster general in President Woodrow Wilson's cabinet during World War I. Burleson prevented newspapers he thought were disloyal to the war effort from being sent through the mail.

about what they could print. (To a certain extent during all wars, the American news media willingly hold back information from the public—for example, about the number and movements of soldiers in a battle.) Because of this, the mainstream media were not usually censored. Although Congress had passed the law, it was Postmaster General Albert Burleson who decided what publications should be kept from the mail. If a newspaper could not be mailed, it could not reach its readers. Restricting which newspapers could be sent through the mail was, until radio and television came along, an effective way to censor the press.

In general, Burleson censored pacifist, socialist, and other radical newspapers. These often spoke out against the drafting of soldiers, encouraged men not to enlist, and did not support the American war effort. They were targeted because they were opposed politically to government policy, not because they gave away military secrets.

Victor Berger, from Wisconsin, was the first socialist congressman to be elected in the United States. He was also the editor of the *Milwaukee Leader*. Berger spoke out against the war in his newspaper. He was charged three times for breaking the Espionage Act, so the *Leader* could no longer be mailed. Berger also received a twenty-year jail sentence. After he appealed his conviction, his case went to the Supreme Court. In 1921, the Court ruled in his favor. Berger was reelected to Congress in 1922 and served for three more terms.

In 1918, Congress passed the Sedition Act, expanding the Espionage Act. Anyone could be arrested who published "any disloyal, profane, scurrilous or abusive language about the form of government of the United States, or the Constitution." Before the act was passed, proponents of press freedom expressed disapproval. "The chief criticism was directed against sections of the bill intended to create a censorship on news," reported the *Bridgeport Evening Farmer* in Connecticut. "[It] might even prevent . . . views held by those who want to see some way secured after the present war to guard against wars in the future." This seemed a reasonable view, but during wartime, people are fearful of comments that might encourage the enemy. Mainstream papers soon praised the Sedition Act for controlling unpatriotic sentiments. "All seditionists, all loose-tongued critics of the government's war policies had best beware, because the . . . [act] provides the authority that is needed to clip their wings," declared the *Atlanta Constitution*. "The law will do much good, and it can do no injury to any man who speaks and acts the part of a thorough-going American citizen."

After the Sedition Act was passed in 1918, W. A. Rogers created this cartoon depicting Uncle Sam as he rounds up characters dangerous to the government, including spies and traitors. The character at the bottom left is labeled "I. W. W." for the Industrial Workers of the World, a militant labor union. The act also led to the arrest of socialists who distributed printed material against the war effort.

Between 1919 and 1920, some 877 people were convicted under the Sedition Act and other federal laws. Many of these convictions were for speech considered dangerous to the government. People could plead guilty and pay a fine; if they wanted a jury trial and were found guilty, they often went to jail. A man in Illinois was sentenced to two years in jail for saying that Germany and its ally Hungary were "all right" and that he would fight for Germany and its ruler, the kaiser.

When a law seems to go against a principle of the Constitution, the outcome is sometimes decided by the Supreme Court. The Court's opinions have shaped the way Americans interpret freedom of the press. Two important cases arose out of charges based on the Espionage and Sedition Acts and helped to decide the balance between national security and the First Amendment freedoms of speech and the press. Both cases involved distributing antiwar leaflets. The Supreme Court decisions reflected opinions on freedom of expression—free speech as well as freedom of the press.

Socialists Charles Schenck and Elizabeth Baer used the mail to send out leaflets calling for men to resist the draft in a peaceful way. In fact, the headline of the leaflet read "Long Live the Constitution of the United States." The subhead was "Wake Up, America! Your Liberties Are in Danger!" Schenck and Baer felt the war effort, and the draft in particular, violated the Thirteenth Amendment to the Constitution, which prohibited "involuntary servitude" (slavery). "Help us wipe out this stain on the Constitution," said the leaflet. Schenck and Baer were found guilty in the Pennsylvania courts of violating the Espionage Act. They appealed their case to the Supreme Court. The Court unanimously upheld the guilty convictions.

The Supreme Court heard *Schenck v. United States* in 1919. Justice Oliver Wendell Holmes Jr. wrote the decision confirming they were guilty. "We admit that . . . in ordinary time, the defendants . . . would have been within their constitutional rights," Holmes wrote. "But the character of every act depends upon the circumstances in which it was done . . . The most stringent protection of free speech would not protect a man in falsely shouting fire in a theatre and causing a panic . . . The question in every case is whether the words used are used in such circumstances and are of such a nature as to create a clear and present danger that they will bring about the substantive evils that Congress has a right to prevent."

The example Holmes gave, of a man shouting fire in a theater, has continued to be used by courts as a way of measuring whether free expression can cause danger. Holmes defined this as "clear and present danger"—another phrase that has become important in judging how much free speech can be allowed when national security is at stake. For Holmes in this decision, and for many judges who have followed him, the danger of disrupting the government or encouraging violence must be immediate and likely to happen in order for free speech to be limited.

Several months later, Justice Holmes took a different position when he dissented against the majority opinion in the case of *Abrams v. United States*. In 1918, five defendants, including

*Socialists observe May Day, internationally considered
the day to celebrate laborers, with a 1916 parade. Socialists
tended to be against participation in World War I.*

Jacob Abrams, had been convicted under the Sedition Act in the
New York State courts. They had given out leaflets—including
some thrown out a window in New York City to people walking
by—calling for the United States to stop sending troops to Russia
that might halt the progress of the Communist Russian Revolution of 1917. One of these leaflets called for strikes in American
munitions plants making weapons to use in Russia.

None of the leaflets said anything about supporting Germany.
When questioned in court, all the defendants expressed anti-
German sentiments. They supported the American government

against its main enemy. Yet Abrams, who had printed the leaflets, was sentenced by a New York court to twenty years in prison and a $1,000 fine (about $21,000 in today's currency). Two of his colleagues received the same sentence and two others shorter sentences. Abrams and his fellow defendants appealed their case to the Supreme Court.

Seven members of the Court upheld their guilty convictions. Justice John Clarke wrote, "Even if their [the defendants'] primary purpose and intent was to aid the cause of the Russian Revolution, the plan of action they adopted necessarily involved . . . defeat of the war program of the United States . . . The plain purpose of their propaganda was to excite . . . disaffection, sedition, riots, and, as they hoped, revolution in this country." The majority found evidence of a "clear and present danger."

Holmes did not believe that these leaflets were a real threat. "The principle of the right to free speech is always the same," he wrote. "It is only the present danger of immediate evil or an intent to bring it about that warrants Congress in setting a limit to the expression of opinion . . . Congress certainly cannot forbid all effort to change the mind of the country. Now nobody can suppose that the surreptitious [secret] publishing of a silly leaflet by an unknown man . . . would present any immediate danger . . . We should be eternally vigilant against attempts to check the expression of opinions that we loathe . . . unless they so imminently threaten immediate interference with the . . . pressing purposes of the law that an immediate check is required to save the country."

Socialists distribute pamphlets in New York City's Union Square in 1908. During World War I, printed materials supporting socialism were censored and several socialists were tried and convicted of violating the Espionage and Sedition Acts.

Holmes dismissed the idea of immediate danger because the leaflets were hardly likely to cause mass strikes or endanger the federal government. Instead, he realized that the majority of the Court ruled against the *Abrams* defendants because they did not like their political ideas.

The Sedition Act was repealed in 1921, after World War I had ended. The Espionage Act remained active. It is still used today to bring charges against people thought to have threatened national security.

In 1923, the Supreme Court heard a third case involving the right to distribute printed material that advocated the overthrow of the government. Benjamin Gitlow was charged in 1919 for distributing a "Left Wing Manifesto" and a paper called *The Revolutionary Age* in New York City and through the mail. Together, these writings asked Americans to establish socialism through continued mass strikes, which could be violent if necessary. Gitlow was arrested for violating New York State's Criminal Anarchy Law and found guilty in a New York court. His case, *Gitlow v. New York*, went to the Supreme Court in 1923 and was decided two years later, in 1925.

The majority of the Court upheld the guilty verdict. "It is a fundamental principle . . . that the freedom of speech and of the press which is secured by the Constitution, does not confer an absolute right to speak or publish, without responsibility, whatever one may choose," wrote Justice Edward Terry Sanford. "A State may punish utterances endangering the foundations of organized government."

As he had in *Abrams v. United States*, Oliver Wendell Holmes Jr. dissented. "It is said that this manifesto was more than a theory, that it was an incitement. Every idea is an incitement. It offers itself for belief and if believed it is acted on . . . The only difference between the expression of an opinion and an incitement . . . is the speaker's enthusiasm for the result." Holmes again believed that there was no likelihood that the publications would cause strikes or endanger national security. It was, in effect, Gitlow's politics—the ideas he expressed—that the Court disliked and voted against.

Gitlow v. New York became one of the most important cases regarding press freedom for another reason. Until then, the

Justice Oliver Wendell Holmes Jr. supported the conviction of socialists in the Supreme Court case Schenck v. United States. *He wrote that free speech would not be acceptable if it created "a clear and present danger" to government. In* Abrams v. United States, *however, he disagreed with the majority of the Court, declaring that the defendants did not seriously threaten the country.*

First Amendment had applied only to the federal government. Congress could not pass a law that violated the right to practice freedom of the press. Each state, however, could pass its own law, limiting press and speech for the same reasons the federal government might: for example, for endangering public safety, or, as in Gitlow's case, for allegedly advocating the overthrow of the government. Before the Civil War, abolitionist newspapers were regularly censored by the southern states, and publications in favor of slavery were censored in the North. These cases did not come before the federal courts.

Gitlow was convicted of violating a New York State law, not a federal law. The Supreme Court decision upheld the state law. For the first time, the Court used the Fourteenth Amendment to the Constitution to decide whether state laws against freedom of the press were valid. The Fourteenth Amendment said that "no state shall make or enforce any law which shall abridge the privileges or immunities of citizens of the United States; nor shall any state deprive any person of life, liberty, or property, without due process of law; nor deny to any person within its jurisdiction the equal protection of the laws." The Supreme Court could find that a state law violated "the privileges or immunities of citizens of the United States," or, as in *Gitlow*, that the state had not violated the citizen's rights. This case dramatically expanded the scope of First Amendment protection.

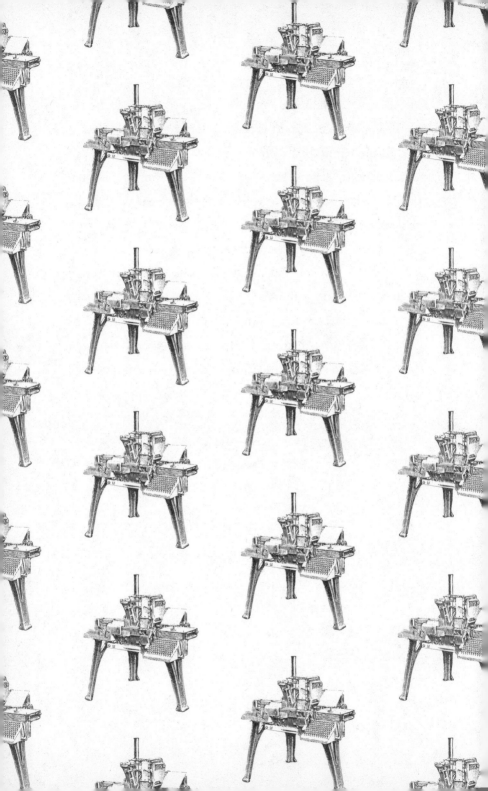

CHAPTER 3

NEWS, POLITICS, AND WAR IN THE NINETEENTH CENTURY

T he nasty campaign in the press between John Adams and Thomas Jefferson for the 1800 presidency was not the last. In 1828, John Adams's son, John Quincy Adams, who served as president from 1825 to 1829, was running for a second term. His opponent was Andrew Jackson, a military hero who had defeated the British army at New Orleans in 1815, during the War of 1812. John Quincy Adams didn't own slaves, but Jackson did. This did not count against him in 1828. Presidents George Washington, Thomas Jefferson, James Madison, and James Monroe had also owned slaves. But Jackson was accused of being a slave trader in the pro-Adams press. In the South, selling slaves was considered a necessary, but low and demeaning, job. "There is no charge which ought to affect more seriously the reputation . . . of General Jackson than that of speculating in slaves," wrote the Washington, D.C., *Daily National Journal*. "Could the people of the U. States . . . elevate to the first office in the nation a man who had been engaged in carrying slaves from one State to

This lithograph shows Andrew Jackson, who vied for the presidency with John Quincy Adams in a vicious campaign in 1828. Jackson was elected the seventh president of the United States.

another, for the purposes of . . . profit, ages would be insufficient to wipe away the foul stain from the annals of our republic."

Often the battle of opinions pro and con against presidents and politicians is between newspapers themselves, not the people being attacked. Pro-Jackson newspapers both praised and defended him. "The man, who, as Mr. Jefferson said, has filled the measure of his country's glory, has been the object of their unceasing and most slanderous attacks. He who achieved the greatest victory in modern times [at New Orleans] . . . has been called a murderer, a swindler . . . and a traitor, because the people have selected him as their Candidate for President," declared *Signs of the Times*, a newspaper in Albany, New York.

Jackson was portrayed as a man of the people, more democratic than Adams. Jackson supporters said that Adams was an elitist and a snob, just as critics had said about his father. He was accused of keeping a billiards table in the White House, an expensive luxury. He was even accused of having the government pay for it. Adams did play billiards, but apparently paid for the table himself. The pro-Jackson press also went after Adams's wife, Louisa, who was born in England. She was considered a foreigner who did not care about the United States.

Adams did not participate in the campaign battle of words, but Jackson did. He wrote to newspaper editors that supported him, giving them advice on how to refute what Adams supporters were writing. He also suggested how they could attack Adams. Jackson won the presidential election by a large majority. As president, he saw the press could be an ally. He gave speeches that appealed to the common man, winning more press coverage than any president before him. He gave a nod to press freedom when he stated a year after he was elected, "As long as our government is administered for the good of the people, and is regulated by their will; as long as it secures to us the rights of persons and of property, liberty of conscience and of the press, it will be worth defending."

Abraham Lincoln was another president who was aware of the power of the press. He served during the Civil War (1861–1865). The Civil War began on April 12, 1861, between the states that had seceded from the United States (the Confederacy) and the Union—the remaining states that fought to preserve the country.

From the beginning of his term, Lincoln was viciously attacked by the southern press, as well as northern newspapers that opposed the war. Only four months after the war started, on August 22, the United States government imposed press censorship. It refused to let the *Daily News* and other New York newspapers that had objected to the war policy be sent to readers through the mail. Three thousand copies of the *Daily News*, which had already reached Philadelphia, were also taken by the federal government to be destroyed.

After the paper was kept from being mailed, publisher Benjamin Wood defended the *News*: "It has abused no privilege as a free press. It has violated no courtesy to the Government . . . by the publication of military facts." If there were an offense, "it . . . is that we have fearlessly . . . exercised the right which the Constitution

This print shows fighting at the First Battle of Bull Run, the first large clash of Union and Confederate troops during the Civil War. Abraham Lincoln, who served as president during the war, received much criticism in the newspapers that opposed his policies.

has guaranteed us, in war as well as in peace, to oppose, not the Government, but the policy of the National Administration [Lincoln and his advisors]." The *News* was right, but it was not a position popular with supporters of the Union.

During the Civil War there was a very partisan press. Lincoln was a Republican—the beginning of what became today's party—and his opponents were Democrats. Some Democrats believed that Lincoln should make peace with the seceding states and, if necessary, let them form their own country. Since the *Daily News* was pro-Democratic, it was opposed not only by the government but also by pro-Republican newspapers that defended Lincoln's

FASTER PRINTERS, FASTER NEWS

In the time between Andrew Jackson's inauguration and Abraham Lincoln's, the number of copies a press could print in a short time increased dramatically, thanks to new technological inventions. The steam-powered rotary press was first used to print a newspaper in London in 1814. Steam power replaced the backbreaking work of printing by hand. In a rotary press, the type was placed on a cylinder instead of a flatbed. Since the cylinder rotated or rolled over the paper, it produced results much faster. In the United States, Thomas Howe created a more advanced model of the steam-powered rotary press in 1843. It was possible to print about twenty thousand copies of a page per hour. By 1861, a city newspaper like the *New York Herald* turned out more than one hundred thousand newspapers a day.

In the 1840s, development of the telegraph by Samuel Morse and other inventors revolutionized the way news could be sent across long distances. The telegraph worked by sending electronic signals representing letters of the alphabet over a wire laid between two places. The telegraph operator tapped a key to spell out messages in "Morse code." This code used a system of dots and dashes to represent each letter of the alphabet and numbers. In 1846, five New York City newspapers formed the Associated Press, which used fast horses, boats, and, of course, the telegraph to quickly transmit news of the Mexican-American War. In 1861, Western Union linked the first telegraph line to stretch across the United States. The telegraph kept western and midwestern states informed about the Civil War.

During the Civil War, newspapers sent correspondents to report on battles—about 350 correspondents came from northern papers and 150 from the South. They could observe and write their stories and telegraph the results to their home newspapers, where they would appear the next day, even in distant locations.

Lithography, a type of printing that became common in the 1830s, made it cheaper and easier for newspapers and news magazines to print pictures. *Litho* means "stone" in Latin, and *graph* is a mark. The process involved writing or drawing an image with a greasy crayon onto limestone.

The crayon was made from a mixture including wax and soap. Ink was then rolled over the stone, only picking up the greasy image and not the background. The same stone could be used over and over to produce many copies. Lithography was mainly used, however, to print pictures, not news, until the late nineteenth century.

Although photography was also used as early as the 1830s to capture images, the technology was not yet available for newspapers to print them directly. During the Civil War, artists copied photographs to be printed with lithography. Newspapers and news magazines also sent artists out to accompany the army and send back sketches, which were also copied by engravers to be printed in large numbers.

THE BATTLE OF GETTYSBURG, Pa JULY 3d 1863.

This lithograph, published by Currier and Ives, probably in 1863, demonstrates the new printing technique that allowed newspapers and news magazines to produce many copies of the same image.

policies. "Certain journals," wrote the *New-York Tribune*, were "just now loud in their eulogies of the freedom of the press" but "equally loud in their sympathy for the Rebels with whom the country is at war." They were "abusing the sacred right guaranteed to all men by the Constitution."

Just as they did to loyalist presses during the Revolutionary War, mobs attacked and destroyed pro-Democratic newspaper offices and damaged their presses. They also tarred and feathered editors who had written against Lincoln's policies. In the summer of 1861, mobs, government agencies, and sometimes Union troops harassed about two hundred newspapers. Some of the editors were held in jail at a Union fort in Brooklyn, New York.

In September 1862, Lincoln stirred up more controversy by announcing the Emancipation Proclamation. This would free the slaves in Confederate territory and allow African Americans to serve in the military. Emancipation was scheduled to go into effect on January 1, 1863. Some Republican newspapers enthusiastically supported Lincoln. The *New York Times* reported on September 25 that "the city [of Washington, D.C.] was enlivened . . . by a serenade to the President, in token of satisfaction with his proclamation. The crowd formed with a band of music . . . and marched with continually increasing numbers to the White House . . . vociferously cheering all loyal and Anti-Slavery sentiments."

Pro-Democratic newspapers, however, were loud in their criticism. The *New York World* called the preliminary Emancipation Proclamation "bloody" and "barbarous" and "adrift on a current

And by virtue of the power and for the purpose aforesaid. I do order and declare that all persons held as SLAVES, within designated States and parts of States are, and henceforward SHALL BE FREE! (excerpt from)

FREEDOM FOR ALL, BOTH BLACK AND WHITE!

EMANCIPATION.

Abraham Lincoln issued the preliminary Emancipation Proclamation in September 1862. It called for freeing the slaves held in Confederate territory. The proclamation went into effect on January 1, 1863. The action was scathingly criticized in the South, and even in some northern newspapers that believed the Union should make peace with the Confederacy.

of racial fanaticism." The *New York Journal of Commerce* wrote, "We have only anticipation of evil from it, and we regard it, as will an immense majority of the people of the North, with profound regret."

Even some papers that had supported Lincoln doubted that former slaves could succeed as free men and women. "If the Proclamation makes the slaves actually free, there will come the further duty of making them work," wrote the *New York Times* on January 3, 1863. "If the slaves choose to 'labor faithfully for reasonable wages'—very well:—they will establish their claim to freedom by the highest titles . . . But if they do not, they must be compelled to do it,—not by brute force . . . but by just and equal laws,—such laws as in every community . . . forbid

Union general Ambrose Burnside (center), shown with staff officers in Virginia, believed that press criticism was only a right in times of peace. He forbade the anti-Lincoln Chicago Times *to publish, but his order was overturned.*

vagrancy . . . and all the shapes by which idle vagabondage preys upon industry and thrift." Racism was strong in the Union, as well as in the Confederacy.

Union general Ambrose Burnside believed that any criticism of Lincoln was wrong. "Newspapers were full of treasonous expression," he stated. He issued an order that charged, "On account of the repeated expression of disloyal and incendiary sentiments, the publication of the newspaper known as the *Chicago Times* is hereby suppressed." A federal court ruled against Burnside's order, but he paid no attention to it for three days. "Freedom of discussion and criticism," he said, were only "proper . . . in time of peace." Lincoln himself gave the order for the *Chicago Times* to publish again.

Lincoln was often tolerant of press criticism in the early years of the war. He was skilled at letting newspapers compete against each other's views rather than his own. He was called a "tyrant," a "butcher," a "monster," a "liar," and an "ignoramus" by various newspapers without having them censored or their editors punished. But in May 1864, two newspapers printed a false proclamation, said to be by Lincoln, calling for a huge increase in Union troops and a possible military draft. Thus provoked, the president gave an order to his military commander in New York for the "Arrest and Imprisonment of Irresponsible Newspaper Reporters and Editors."

> Whereas there has been wickedly and traitorously . . . published this morning in the *New York World* and *New York Journal of Commerce* . . . a false and spurious proclamation purporting to be signed by the President . . . which publication is of a treasonable nature . . . you are therefore hereby commanded forthwith to arrest and imprison . . . the editors, proprietors, and publishers of the aforesaid newspapers . . . and you will hold the persons so arrested in close custody until they can be brought to trial before a military commission for their offense. You will also take possession by military force of the printing establishments of the *New York World* and *Journal of Commerce* . . . and prohibit any further publication therefrom.

This was Lincoln's strongest reaction to the pro-Democratic press. Like Thomas Jefferson, despite friendly press, Lincoln showed increased frustration with opposition newspapers and

TECHNOLOGY LEAPS FORWARD AGAIN

Linotype—"line-of-type"—developed in the late nineteenth century, was the first automatic typesetting machine. Instead of setting only one letter at a time by hand, an operator set type by the line, using a ninety-character keyboard. Molten lead was then poured into the line to create what was called a "slug," the line of metal type used to print the page. The fastest linotype operators could type ten to thirty words a minute.

In 1895, brothers Charles and Alfred Harris developed and sold the first printing press that automatically fed paper through the machine, instead of feeding it by hand. Their invention meant paper could be passed through ten times faster than the traditional way.

In 1904, Ira Rubel, a paper manufacturer from New Jersey, discovered offset printing. He used a flat stone covered with a rubber cylinder meant to transfer the image from stone to paper. Sometimes the image got printed on the cylinder rather than the paper. This image turned out to be clearer than the one directly printed on paper. Rubel created a press where the image was printed directly from the cylinder, not the stone. Because the cylinder could be rolled quickly around and around, offset printing was much faster than plain lithography.

Linotype operators are at work at the New York World *in 1909. The first automatic typesetting machine, linotype revolutionized the printing of newspapers.*

their opinions. As the Civil War drew to a close in April 1865, however, formal censorship policies were no longer necessary.

But during the war the press itself changed. In cities where there was more than one newspaper, competition kept them alert for ways to increase sales. Although ads had appeared in eighteenth-century newspapers, in the nineteenth century, newspapers increasingly relied on making more money by selling advertisements; the more readers a newspaper had, the more advertisers wanted their products in the paper. Newspapers were businesses, and income, as well as political opinions, influenced what they wrote.

By the 1890s, two New York newspapers had become well known for their rivalry over readers: the *New York World*, owned by Joseph Pulitzer, and the *New York Journal*, owned by William Randolph Hearst.

They exaggerated stories to make them more exciting. They used ever bigger, more dramatic headlines and type. They wanted news to be sensational and shocking, to provoke readers' curiosity and eagerness to keep up with the most current disasters. They did not care about factual reporting or whether a story was true. Their style became known as "yellow journalism." The name came from a cartoon character, the Yellow Kid. His clothes stood out in the black-and-white newspapers because the big nightshirt he wore was printed in yellow ink.

The Yellow Kid was a character from the comic strip *Hogan's Alley*. He was a boy from the New York slums with a feisty attitude. The cartoon was aimed at adults. Underneath the often slapstick humor, it revealed the problems of class and race in the city. The *World* ran the Yellow Kid first, then the *Journal* took it over.

Editor Erwin Wardman appears to be the first to use the term "yellow journalism," in the 1890s. He called it "yellow-kid journalism," but the term got shortened. He was upset that newspapers like the *World* and the *Journal* were using cartoons, instead of news coverage, to draw readers. Other newspapers besides these two practiced yellow journalism, but some did not. They wanted to emphasize truthful, carefully reported news. But the *World* and the *Journal*, which sold for as little as one penny an issue, were extremely popular.

In 1897 and 1898, the Spanish colony of Cuba was fighting for its freedom from Spain. At first, news of the Cuban revolution did not appear regularly in the American press. The *World*

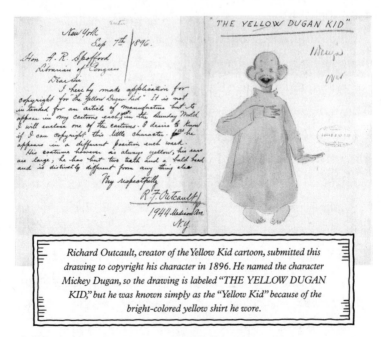

Richard Outcault, creator of the Yellow Kid cartoon, submitted this drawing to copyright his character in 1896. He named the character Mickey Dugan, so the drawing is labeled "THE YELLOW DUGAN KID," but he was known simply as the "Yellow Kid" because of the bright-colored yellow shirt he wore.

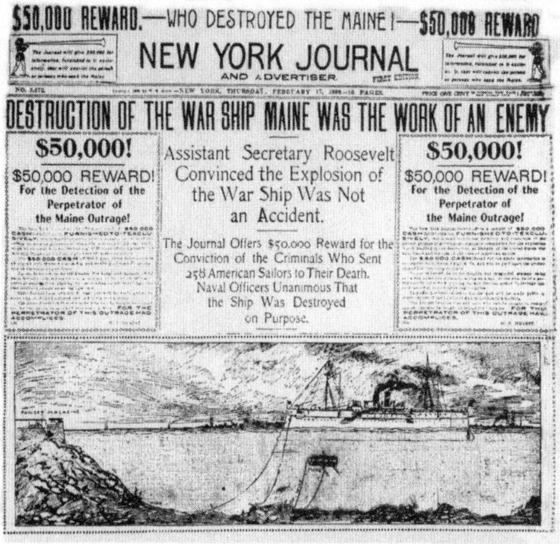
$50,000 REWARD.—WHO DESTROYED THE MAINE!—$50,000 REWARD

NEW YORK JOURNAL

AND ADVERTISER

DESTRUCTION OF THE WAR SHIP MAINE WAS THE WORK OF AN ENEMY

$50,000!

$50,000 REWARD!
For the Detection of the Perpetrator of the Maine Outrage!

Assistant Secretary Roosevelt Convinced the Explosion of the War Ship Was Not an Accident.

The Journal Offers $50,000 Reward for the Conviction of the Criminals Who Sent 258 American Sailors to Their Death. Naval Officers Unanimous That the Ship Was Destroyed on Purpose.

$50,000!

$50,000 REWARD!
For the Detection of the Perpetrator of the Maine Outrage!

This giant front-page headline appeared in the New York Journal *on February 17, 1898. The* Journal *accused Spain of destroying the battleship* Maine*, although this was not true. The* Journal *and other "yellow press" newspapers used boldly printed, shocking headlines and subheads, graphic boxes, and illustrations to make their coverage of events more sensational.*

and the *Journal* became more interested in covering it when, on February 15, 1898, the battleship U.S.S. *Maine* exploded in the harbor of Cuba's capital, Havana. Two hundred and sixty Americans were killed.

By February 17, the front-page headline of the *Journal* read: "Destruction of the War Ship *Maine* Was the Work of an Enemy." The paper offered a $50,000 reward (about $1.5 million in today's currency) for the name of whoever had caused the explosion. The *World*'s front-page headline on the same day was more cautious: "*Maine* Explosion Caused by Bomb or Torpedo?" It reported that Charles Sigsbee, commander of the *Maine*, said in a telegram sent to Washington, D.C.: "The Accident Was Made Possible by an Enemy." No one has ever been sure what caused the accident, although it almost certainly was not the Spanish. But by April 1898, partly encouraged by the press coverage, the United States was at war with Spain in Cuba.

The Spanish-American War was short. It ended on August 13, with a victory for the United States. The press coverage, however,

American soldiers fire on a fort at El Caney, Cuba, in 1898, during the Spanish-American War. Newspapers sent reporters to travel with the U.S. Army, who sent their stories by telegram to the United States.

was intense. American newspapers sent correspondents to travel with the U.S. Army. They sent their stories back by telegram, which appeared in their newspapers the next day. Although there was government censorship, the censors could not keep up with the news. In fact, they often used the press to gather information.

Some newspaper correspondents made the war seem romantic and a test of manly courage. "The firing-drill of the marines was splendid," wrote Stephen Crane for the *New York Herald*. "The men reloaded and got up their guns like lightening, but afterward there was always a rock-like beautiful poise as the aim was taken . . . As for daring . . . they paid no heed whatever to the Spaniards' volleys of ammunition." Such reporting ignored the misery and loss of life in battles.

After Spain lost the war, the United States was set to take over the Philippines, another Spanish colony in the Pacific. Filipinos who wanted complete independence rebelled and fought from

1899 to 1902 in what became known as the Philippine-American War. American soldiers, many of them volunteers and from rural areas, sent home letters to their families expressing doubts about fighting against a much less powerful country. Small-town newspapers printed these letters, encouraging antiwar sentiment in the United States.

Eventually, there was a backlash against yellow journalism. By the end of the nineteenth century, some newspaper editors and members of the public were tired of the kind of "news" that ignored correct information. They wanted reporting that was objective—based on facts that could be proved and not on opinion or imagination. Such a newspaper would not be influenced by pressure from politicians or advertisers to ignore what was negative but true.

When Adolph Ochs took over the *New York Times* in 1896, it was not competing well with the *World*, the *Journal*, and other yellow press newspapers. Ochs wanted a different kind of newspaper. He declared in an announcement in the *Times* on August 18, 1896, that his newspaper would be "clean, dignified, trustworthy and impartial," for "thoughtful, pure-minded people." Many doubted this model would succeed. In fact, Ochs almost went bankrupt. He lowered the price to a penny to compete with the yellow press, a great risk in terms of the newspaper's income. But for the same price they would pay for the *World* and the *Journal*, New Yorkers were apparently happy to get the *Times*. The public seemed seriously interested in reporting grounded in facts.

Adolph Ochs began publishing the New York Times *in 1896, turning it into a responsible, carefully reported newspaper. He is shown here with his daughter Iphigene, who was ten years old at the time. She later married Arthur Sulzberger, who took over as the* Times' *publisher in 1935.*

The role of the reporter developed throughout the twentieth century. He or she came to depend on reliable sources. Whether government agencies, the military, or a witness to an event, these sources had direct experience with what had happened. The reporters used hard evidence: for example, written reports from the government, or photographs, instead of just hearsay, to back up their statements. Editorial opinions were still included in fact-based newspapers. But what the public increasingly relied upon for accurate information were the news stories.

Mainstream newspapers like the *New York Times*, the *Wall Street Journal*, the *Los Angeles Times*, the *Boston Globe*, the *Chicago Tribune*, and the *Washington Post* built reputations on the accuracy of their reporting. Readers came to count on them for reliable news accounts. But these newspapers did have their points of view. Editorials for the *Wall Street Journal*, for example, tended to be conservative, while the *Washington Post* was seen as liberal. Newspapers could control information by printing what they wanted to—or not informing the public about views they disagreed with. The most heavily censored media throughout the twentieth century, however, were communist or fascist publications that took more radical political stands. But because of freedom of the press, even the views and opinions of a small minority were usually available for the public to read.

Investigative journalism developed at the end of the nineteenth century. This was a way of reporting that involved deep and long-lasting focus on a newsworthy topic. It might take months, or even years, for a reporter to assemble all the facts and evidence that would make his or her case. However, it often exposed lies and corruption.

Beginning in about 1890, a group of writers dedicated themselves to investigating political and economic corruption. They went after racist practices, business monopolies, poverty, unfair labor practices, and child labor. President Theodore Roosevelt labeled these writers "muckrakers" in a 1906 speech. Roosevelt did believe in some reforms to government and business. "Now it is very necessary that we should not flinch from seeing what is vile and debasing," he said. "There is filth on the floor . . ." But he felt the muckrakers went too far, concentrating only on what was bad. The muckrakers themselves were proud of the nickname and the service to the public they performed.

They included Jacob Riis (1849–1914), a reporter for several New York newspapers. He wrote about the terrible conditions in the slums. He also took powerful photographs that documented the life of the poor. In addition to newspaper articles, Riis published books, including *How the Other Half Lives: Studies Among the Tenements of New York*. Because of his work, the city began to clean up the slums, providing sanitary sewers and collecting garbage for the first time.

Ida B. Wells (1862–1931), an African American journalist and publisher of the *Free Speech and Headlight*, a newspaper in Memphis, Tennessee, was so horrified when three of her friends were lynched that she began a campaign against this form of illegal killing. She investigated statistics and facts, showing that nearly all the people lynched in different parts of the United States were black and often innocent of a crime. She upset white Southerners so much that a mob destroyed her newspaper office and presses. She was forced to move north, where she continued her campaign.

Upton Sinclair (1878–1968) published a novel, *The Jungle*, after researching the meatpacking industry in Chicago. It told the public about health-threatening, unsafe conditions, including descriptions of rotting meat. Americans were outraged. In 1906—the same year Roosevelt coined the term *muckrakers*—Congress passed the Pure Food and Drug Act and the Federal Meat Inspection Act, inspired by Sinclair's work.

Ida Tarbell (1857–1944) was a journalist for *McClure's Magazine*. She looked into the way that John D. Rockefeller and his company, Standard Oil, did business. Tarbell exposed the company's sometimes illegal tactics, preventing smaller companies from competing. She published articles and the book *The History of the Standard Oil Company*. This led to Congress passing the Sherman Antitrust Act against business monopolies.

The muckrakers did not investigate the government directly, but they were watchdogs protecting Americans. Although Ida B. Wells's work never led to a federal law making lynching illegal, the others were able to influence government to pass necessary laws.

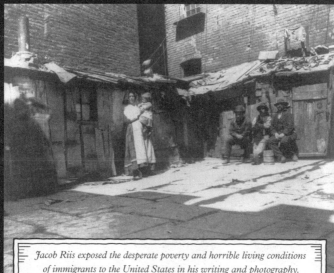

Jacob Riis exposed the desperate poverty and horrible living conditions of immigrants to the United States in his writing and photography. This 1888 photograph of a yard in a New York City slum movingly illustrated Riis's view of their plight.

CHAPTER 4

TWENTIETH-CENTURY PRESIDENTS, WAR, AND THE NEWS MEDIA

I n November 1916, a few thousand Americans learned the news that Woodrow Wilson had defeated Charles Evans Hughes for president. They didn't read it in a newspaper. They heard it broadcast on the radio by Lee de Forest, an inventor who, in 1906, had improved the new technology. Only a handful of people owned radios. The broadcast reached only two hundred miles. But by the middle of the twentieth century, most American homes had radios, radio stations reached the entire country, and radio was an important medium for conveying the news.

Between 1920 and 1921, thirty radio stations began operating in the United States. Station 8MK (later WWJ) in Detroit was the first to broadcast news. (It was also the first station owned by a newspaper, the *Detroit News*.) On August 31, 1920, it told listeners the results of a local election. By November, KDKA in Pittsburgh was reporting the results of the presidential election,

RADIO DELIVERS THE NEWS

Inventors were working on a way to send sound over a distance using electromagnetic waves (instead of electrical wires) in the 1890s. The device they produced was called radio. Nikola Tesla did some early work on radio waves in the United States, including the development of an electrical transmitter. Italian Guglielmo Marconi, working in England, is credited with sending and receiving the first wireless message across the Atlantic Ocean in 1901. In 1912, Edwin Armstrong created a device to amplify the wave, making the sound louder.

Congress became involved in radio broadcasting in 1912, passing the first government regulations for radio stations. These were commercial ventures that reached large audiences. Some regulation was necessary because there were only a limited number of broadcast frequencies. Radio waves needed to travel through the air, and if too many were on the same frequency, they interrupted each other. These regulations had nothing to do with the content of news broadcasts, since the earliest radio broadcasts featured music, not news. But during World War I, which ended in November 1918, the American government kept radio from broadcasting at all as a security measure.

won by Warren Harding. In between election returns and music, it broadcast the message: "Will anyone hearing this broadcast please communicate with us, as we are anxious to know how far the broadcast is reaching and how it is being received." Hundreds of Americans sent postcards to the station to confirm that they were listening.

Radio began broadcasting regular news in the 1920s. Much of what announcers read came from print newspapers. But Americans appreciated the way radio brought events right into their homes, making them seem more immediate. Realizing how popular radio news had become, stations started sending out their own reporters.

The rise to power of Adolf Hitler and the Nazi Party in Germany in the 1930s created

An American family
listens to their radio
sometime around 1940.
Early radios were often
large and solid, like
pieces of furniture. People
gathered around them
to hear entertainment
and news.

THE RADIO AUDIENCE, U.S.A., LISTENS TO THE NEWS

great interest about whether Europe would go to war. British diplomats met with Nazi representatives in Munich in September 1938. The meetings ended in a compromise. American radio stations provided around-the-clock coverage. H. V. Kaltenborn of CBS's radio news network made 102 broadcasts in two and a half weeks. He not only presented the facts but was known for his analysis of politics. Sales of radio sets shot up.

During World War II (1939–1945), Americans gathered around their radios to hear the news. CBS featured Edward R. Murrow, the most famous news broadcaster of the time. CBS also had reporters in other European cities. They sent in live reports by shortwave radio during Murrow's broadcasts, an immediacy that print newspapers could not match. Radio had much the same impact on the way Americans received and interpreted news that the internet has today.

The First Amendment applied to radio news broadcasts, as it did to printed news. But during World War II, the American

Franklin D. Roosevelt, thirty-second president of the United States, delivers a Fireside Chat on September 6, 1936. His weekly radio broadcasts kept America informed about his policies and national and international events through the years of World War II.

government had no major conflicts with radio. In fact, mainstream radio not only broadcast a weekly program by President Franklin D. Roosevelt, the "Fireside Chats," but inspired patriotism with the rest of its coverage. However, the government eventually sought some censorship of the news.

When the United States entered World War II in 1941, radio was as important a part of press coverage as print newspapers. Although Europe and Asia had been at war for two years, the

United States joined only after Japanese forces attacked Pearl Harbor in Hawaii on December 7, 1941. The issue of press freedom versus national security again became important. President Franklin Roosevelt issued an order setting up an Office of Censorship on December 19. Byron Price, a news editor at the Associated Press, agreed to lead it.

"To a free people, the very word 'censorship' always has been distasteful," Price explained. "Yet even the . . . [loudest] critics of the principle of censorship agree that in war-time some form and amount . . . is a necessity." The Office of Censorship issued a "Code of Wartime Practices for the American Press" on January 15, 1942. What made it unusual was that it was voluntary. "This Code does not order papers to print or to withhold anything . . . It lists the types of information which the Government feels should be omitted for the effective prosecution of the war, and asks the cooperation of the papers. Thus, every editor, every copy-reader, every reporter and writer, becomes his own censor."

Radio broadcasters were also asked to follow censorship guidelines. So were the makers of newsreels—short films

Newsreel photographers film an event at the White House in the late 1930s. Short newsreels featuring current events appeared before the main feature in movie theaters. Newsreels, as well as newspapers, followed censorship guidelines during World War II.

about newsworthy events shown before the main feature in a movie theater. "It is a heartening example of democracy at work," Price stated. "In no other nation is radio operating under so liberal a program. In no other nation does the press retain so much of its peace-time freedom; there is no censorship of opinion, providing, of course, that statements are not seditious." He did not mention that the Espionage Act of 1917 was still in place.

Mainstream media stuck to the guidelines, but fascist, pro-German publications were prosecuted.

 A **FASCIST** government promotes nationalism. It favors people whose ancestors are from the country, with the same religion and culture, rather than immigrants. It suppresses any kind of disagreement. The fascist, pro-Nazi press was violently anti-Semitic and blamed Jewish influence for the United States entering the war.

William Dudley Pelley published fascist writings in his magazine, *Roll Call*. In another magazine, *The Galilean*, Pelley had written, "To rationalize that the United States got into the war because of an unprovoked attack on Pearl Harbor, is fiddle-faddle." He declared, "Mr. President . . . might, easily . . . have prevented the attack," and added, "We have by every act and deed performable, aggressively solicited war with . . . [Japan and Germany]." In 1942, Pelley was arrested and convicted of sedition. He was sentenced to fifteen years in prison but was paroled after eight years.

Father Charles Coughlin speaks to a rally in Cleveland, Ohio, on May 10, 1936. He was a well-known radio personality who opposed the policies of President Roosevelt and who spread anti-Semitic sentiments until 1942, when the Catholic Church ordered him to stop broadcasting political opinions.

Also in 1942, postal officials banned the mailing of *Social Justice*, a publication of the far-right radio personality Father Charles Coughlin. He was totally opposed to the Roosevelt administration and was aggressively anti-Semitic. "When we get through with the Jews in America, they'll think the treatment they received in Germany was nothing," Coughlin said. Coughlin was a Catholic priest, but his views were not supported by Catholic leaders. In 1942, as the federal government considered bringing a charge of sedition against him, his bishop ordered him to stop all political activities, and he did.

On the other side of the political spectrum, *The Militant*, the journal of the Socialist Workers Party, was also banned from the mails. Socialist and pacifist publications had been heavily censored in World War I. During World War II, Postmaster General Frank C. Walker said that *The Militant* tried "to embarrass and defeat the government in its effort to prosecute the war." William O'Brien, the Post Office attorney, declared, "We believe that anyone violates the Espionage Act who holds up and dwells on the horrors of war with the effect that enlistment is discouraged." Before 1942 ended, about thirty publications were banned from the mail.

The American government also censored photographs and film footage. They did not want pictures published that showed the dead bodies of soldiers or any violent scene that might upset American civilians. In combat zones, censorship was not voluntary. Photos taken there were vigorously reviewed prior to publication. The process consisted of a system of field censors and further review by the War Department's Bureau of Public Relations in Washington, D.C. The types of photos that were censored included civilian victims of American firepower and GIs who committed atrocities, as well as enemy soldiers being treated by American medics.

Exposed to a continuing stream of stories on the bravery and spirit of American soldiers, Americans at home were protected from the brutal realities of the war. By 1943, the public had lost some of its enthusiasm for supporting the war effort. The

This photograph of dead American soldiers at Buna Beach, New Guinea, appeared in Life *magazine in September 1943. It was the first photo of dead American troops to appear in a periodical in the United States. Before this, photographs that showed the grim realities of war were censored by the American military.*

federal Office of War Information realized that not showing images of wounded or dead soldiers led Americans to believe that "some get hurt and ride smiling in aerial ambulances, but that none of them get badly shot or spill any blood." In May 1943, the office released photographs of wounded troops, which appeared in *Newsweek*. In September, *Life* magazine published a photo of three dead American soldiers lying on a beach in the Pacific. The placement of these photos showed that, although there is always censorship during wars, the government also needs the media to tell Americans what it wants them to know. No matter how much tension or disagreement there is between media and government, privately run newspapers, radio stations, and, later, television stations were the ways the government reached the public before the internet.

During the Korean War (1950–1953), the mainstream press began to give less than full support to government policy. After World War II, the country of Korea was divided, with two separate governments. North Korea was Communist, supported by Communist China and the Soviet Union. South Korea was supported by the United States. When North Korean troops

A patrol of American soldiers is pinned down by Chinese Communist forces in northeast Korea in 1950. Military losses in Korea affected reports in American newspapers, where some journalists began to question whether the United States could win the war.

attacked South Korea in 1950, the United Nations responded by sending in troops from twenty-one countries. The United States provided 90 percent of the military forces.

In the beginning months, when neither side appeared to be winning, the American press voluntarily cooperated with the government in covering the war. In fact, many applauded the effort to halt the spread of Communism. "We have drawn a line, not across the [Korean] peninsula, but across the world," said Edward R. Murrow in a CBS News broadcast. "We have concluded that Communism has passed beyond the use of [political] subversion to conquer independent nations and will now use armed invasion and war. And we . . . have demonstrated that we are prepared to . . . face the prospect of war rather than let it happen."

However, as months went by, some newspaper reports began to detail American losses. "In the past week Red [Communist] tanks have raced against crumbling South Korean opposition and have overrun several American positions," wrote an Associated Press correspondent on July 6, 1950. "A key American command post was evacuated before the Communists' armored drive. Soldiers left behind to fight a rear guard action were outflanked as the Reds came on . . . When asked by a correspondent whether the situation was bad or good . . . [an American commander] replied: 'No situation is good unless you are advancing.'"

Marguerite Higgins, a correspondent for the *New York Herald Tribune*, wrote of an American retreat from a battle near Cheonan, Korea, after the soldiers were trapped by Communist forces. "The

Correspondent Marguerite Higgins, typewriter on her lap, adjusts her helmet as she prepares to report on the Korean War. Higgins was a correspondent for the New York Herald Tribune *and a pioneer female journalist.*

bedraggled soldiers, some in a daze from lack of sleep, were violent in denouncing the position they had been put in and it was commonplace to hear the phrase, 'It wasn't a battle, but a slaughter.'"

The media also began criticizing American military officers and their strategy. "Correspondents are not supposed to criticize command decisions," said Edward R. Murrow, after he had spent six weeks in Korea, in a CBS broadcast on August 8, 1950. "But there are responsible officers out there who doubt that we can afford the luxury of attacking in the south [of Korea] when we are so thin on the ground."

Upset by such criticism, General Douglas MacArthur, commander in chief of the forces in Korea, ordered in December 1950 that censorship was no longer voluntary. The new system required reporters to clear their stories with the military. Those in Korea who sent embarrassing articles to their newspapers and radio and television stations could be suspended or deported from Korea. Nearly two dozen reporters were expelled. Those who brought their stories back to the United States, however, could publish them without censorship. Censorship by the military in Korea continued through the end of the war in 1953.

The experience in Korea caused the news media to question the need for total censorship. Some of the stories and photographs censored did not qualify as protecting national security. Instead, they were censored to keep Americans from knowing the harsher, more deadly realities of war. Press freedom called for publishing both the good and the bad so that people could make up their own minds about how war was progressing. After Korea, an increasing number of reporters no longer trusted the government to provide full and accurate details of events and policies.

CHAPTER 5

CIVIL RIGHTS, VIETNAM, AND THE NEWS MEDIA

A s the Korean War drew to a close, the civil rights movement to end racial segregation in the South was gaining national attention in the 1950s and 1960s. At the same time, the United States was being drawn further into a war in Vietnam (1955–1975), between a Communist government in the north and an American-backed government in the south. In both instances, the press covered actions that were controversial. Both involved cases that ended with the Supreme Court setting standards for future cases involving freedom of the press.

Saying that national security is at risk is one way to justify press censorship. Another barrier to press freedom is libel. Libel is the publishing of a false story that says negative things about a person, which might ruin his or her good reputation. Both government officials and ordinary citizens can claim libel.

On March 29, 1960, the *New York Times* ran a full-page ad submitted to them by the Committee to Defend Martin Luther King and the Struggle for Freedom in the South. The committee

WATER
DEPARTMENT

Martin Luther King Jr. is taken to a hearing by Alabama policemen on October 1, 1960, charged with violating probation. As a leader of the civil rights movement, King was indicted or jailed several times in the South.

formed to raise money for the legal defense of King, who had been charged in Alabama with lying about his tax returns. The committee also wanted to support student sit-ins to integrate all-white lunch counters and other student demonstrations. The ad gave examples of southern cities where protests had taken place. It pointed out the aggressive response of white officials, including the police, to stop the protests. One of these was in Montgomery, where, the ad said, "police armed with shotguns and tear-gas ringed the Alabama State College Campus" to keep students from demonstrating.

L. B. Sullivan was a Montgomery official who headed the city's police. He was not mentioned by name in the ad, nor was anybody else. But he sued the *New York Times* for libel, claiming that people knew he was the one in charge and therefore the ad had hurt his reputation. He did not sue the committee that had placed the ad.

During the trial that took place in an Alabama State court, it came out that the ad included details that were incorrect. For example, police did not form a ring around the campus but stayed to one side. The ad said that black students demonstrating on the steps of the state capitol sang "My Country, 'Tis of Thee"; they had actually sung "The Star-Spangled Banner." The *Times* admitted that there were minor mistakes. The paper might be negligent—although this was an ad, not a news report—but it had not deliberately printed false information. In any case, the mistakes had nothing to do with Sullivan himself. But the jury found the *Times* guilty of libel. They awarded Sullivan $500,000. The Alabama appeals court upheld the decision.

This was the largest amount for damages ever awarded by an Alabama court. Three more Montgomery officials and the governor of Alabama decided to also sue for libel. If they won, and the *Times* had to pay everyone such large amounts, it would be hurt financially. In fact, that was a big reason to bring the libel cases to court: to show northern newspapers that writing about the civil rights movement in the South could open them up to expensive lawsuits. Supporters of segregation did not want civil rights to become a national issue, with public opinion on the side of African Americans.

"Down in our part of the country we wish you Northerners would ease up just a little bit on the pressure," said a Texas newspaper editor in 1956 about northern coverage of desegregation in the South.

Martin Luther King Jr. understood the power of the northern press when he wrote in 1963, "It is terribly difficult to wage such a battle [for civil rights] without the moral support of the national press to counteract the hostility of local editors."

The *Times* appealed to the United States Supreme Court. The case, *New York Times Co. v. Sullivan*, was heard in 1964. The decision for damages was supported by Alabama state law; but *Gitlow v. New York* and other earlier cases had established that the Supreme Court could overrule a state law, following the Fourteenth Amendment. The lawyers for Sullivan stressed the mistakes in the ad. The lawyers for the *Times* argued that the mistakes were minor and not printed with the knowledge

that they were incorrect. They pointed out that the decision in the Alabama courts went against the First Amendment right to criticize the government. What was more important: Sullivan's "official reputation" or the constitutional protection of "freedom of political expression"?

The Supreme Court ruled unanimously in favor of the *New York Times*. "We consider this case against the background of a profound national commitment to the principle that debate on public issues should be uninhibited, robust, and wide-open, and that it may well include vehement, caustic, and sometimes unpleasantly sharp attacks on government and public officials," wrote Justice William Brennan Jr. "The present advertisement, as an expression of grievance and protest on one of the major public issues of our time, would seem clearly to qualify for the constitutional protection." Brennan wrote that the public need for information was more important than some "factual errors."

Brennan was concerned that the press would limit its criticism of government because of "the fear of damage awards under a rule such as that invoked by the Alabama courts." They would censor critical opinions themselves to avoid expensive libel suits. But Brennan stated that a "public official" could recover damages for a false statement only where the error was made with "actual malice"—that is, with knowledge that it was false or with "reckless disregard" of whether it was false or not.

The Supreme Court decision in *New York Times Co. v. Sullivan* upheld freedom of the press at a time when it was important for civil rights leaders to make their case in the North. What northern readers and viewers read in their newspapers showed them the violence and cruelty underlying segregation. This was something that was hidden from them in southern white press coverage, if northern readers read southern newspapers at all.

The difference in reporting was clear, for example, during the civil rights campaign in Birmingham, Alabama, in 1963. There, police set dogs loose on peaceful protesters and sprayed them with high-pressure fire hoses. On May 4, many northern newspapers

*During civil rights demonstrations in Birmingham,
Alabama, on May 4, 1963, police set attack dogs
on African American protesters.*

featured the story on the front page with vivid photographs. "U.S.
Calls on Alabama to Halt Racial Strife," read the huge headline
in the *Detroit News*. But the *Birmingham News* reported on page
two that "about 100 negro demonstrators singing and strutting
were dispersed with fire hoses and police dogs this afternoon as
new marches were attempted." It did not stress how aggressive the
police actions were.

The growing use of television to deliver the news also had
an impact on Americans. Nightly news programs showed large
audiences images of police attacking peaceful protesters.

Headlines on the front page of the Detroit News *on May 4, 1963, highlight the violence used against demonstrators in Birmingham, Alabama, during civil rights demonstrations.*

Many southern newspapers, including the Birmingham News, *barely mention the incidents of police violence. The paper noted, in a slim column mid-page, that Alabama governor George Wallace "deplored" the demonstrations, and then covered the story, stressing the behavior of demonstrators.*

Many white northerners were shocked. "The events in Birmingham . . . have so increased the cries for equality that no city or state or legislative body can prudently choose to ignore them," said President John F. Kennedy. Congress passed the Civil Rights Act in 1964, desegregating public facilities, and the Voting Rights Act in 1965.

David Sarnoff had predicted the power of television to influence audiences as early as 1945. Sarnoff was the president of NBC, which at that time was a radio network. "Television will be a mighty window," he said, "through which people in all walks of life, rich and poor alike, will be able to see themselves, not only the small world around us but the larger world we are a part of." He saw the potential for bringing not only sound but visual images into the home. Sarnoff believed that television would become Americans' "principal source of entertainment, education and news."

The first television program was broadcast by station WRGB in 1928. It was *The Queen's Messenger*, an American play written about a British diplomat and a mysterious

★★★★★ TELEVISION BRINGS THE NEWS HOME

Although there were mechanical televisions in the early twentieth century, the first electronic TV was not invented until 1927. The electronic television had a cathode-ray tube in its body. A cathode ray is a stream of electrons, which have a negative charge. A tiny heated filament—a thin piece of wire—released these electrons toward the TV screen. Copper wire wrapped around "steering coils" created a magnetic field to direct the electrons to the correct place on the screen. There, an anode—a conductor charged with positive electrons—received the negative signals. In order for them to be visible, the screen had to be coated with phosphor, a substance that glows.

Philo T. Farnsworth transmitted the first image on electronic television. He scratched a line on a piece of black-painted glass. He placed the glass between a very bright light and the cathode-ray tube. In the room next door, viewers had a screen with an anode. When Farnsworth turned the black glass in the first room, they could see the line move in the other.

THE TELEVISION RECEIVING SET

A man and woman tune into their television set, sometime in 1940. Early television sets had very small screens and most American homes at the time did not have one.

woman. Fewer than a dozen televisions, perhaps only four, received the broadcast. The screen size was three inches. It wasn't until the late 1930s that more television sets began selling to the American public.

After the United States entered World War II in December 1941, the development of television technology and the manufacturing of sets slowed down. The country put its industrial effort into military equipment and technology. In 1945, there were fewer than ten thousand television sets in American homes.

But by 1962, the number of televisions in the United States had jumped to 52 million. In 2001, the number reached 248 million, and many households had two sets.

Entertainment was a big part of television. Popular programs, like comedies and sports events, brought in the most money from advertising. But news was always a part of programming. In the 1950s, television coverage included the presidential nominating conventions for the Republicans and Democrats. Stations ran film footage from U.S. government and military sources, foreign sources, and news agencies. They increasingly used their own cameramen to film what they showed. The anchorman or -woman—a person sitting behind a desk to present the events of the day—became a feature of news on television.

In 1960, Vice President Richard Nixon, a Republican, and Senator John F. Kennedy, a Democrat, were campaigning against each other to become president of the United States. On September 26, they made political and media history by taking part in the first presidential debate shown live on television. Seventy million Americans watched them. Nixon had been ahead in the polls, but the next day Kennedy held a slight majority. Kennedy eventually won the presidency by a small margin. Many historians felt that his appearance on television made the difference.

Later in the 1960s, television became important for coverage of the Vietnam War. Although television did not cover the most violent clashes, it showed enough violence to affect public opinion. More and more Americans protested against the country's participation in the war. The media's doubts in turn influenced the public.

The United States sent advisory troops to South Vietnam in 1955. In July 1959, the first American soldiers were killed there. Under Presidents Dwight Eisenhower, John Kennedy, Lyndon Johnson, and Richard Nixon, the United States continued to send more troops. The goal, the government told the American people, was to keep Vietnam from becoming Communist. "If, when the chips are down, the world's most powerful nation, the United States of America, acts like a pitiful, helpless giant, the forces of totalitarianism and anarchy will threaten free nations and free institutions throughout the world," Nixon stated in 1970.

After 1960, as the number of American deaths rose, more reporters were sent to Vietnam from major newspapers and television stations. By August 1965, there were 419 accredited members of the press corps in the country. They were stationed

Express *correspondent Terry Fincher (*left*) and Larry Burrows of* Life *magazine are encamped at "Hill Timothy" in Vietnam while covering the Vietnam War in April 1968.*

in Saigon (now Ho Chi Minh City), the South Vietnamese capital, though some ventured into the war zone. The U.S. Military Assistance Command, Vietnam (MACV) tried to control the information the press received. But it also transported journalists who wanted to go to the battlefield to report directly on conditions.

At first the mainstream media did not question the need to be in Vietnam in order to stop the spread of communism. But journalists began sending back more negative stories, includ-

Television journalist Walter Cronkite reports from a bombed-out area in Vietnam in February 1968 for CBS News. During the Vietnam War, reporters like Cronkite had access to American soldiers, although some of their stories were censored by the military.

ing losses by the South Vietnamese army the Americans were there to support. The *New York Times* reported on a January 1963 battle "in which attacking South Vietnamese troops were badly beaten by Communist guerillas . . . United States advisors in the field . . . have long felt that conditions here made a defeat like this virtually inevitable."

Reporters in Vietnam were freer to travel through the country than they had been in previous wars. "We were right with the soldiers—no problem with access whatsoever," said television journalist Walter Cronkite. "We talked to them; they talked to us . . . The military did not make any attempt to monitor the interviews we got with the men."

The media emphasized the bravery of American soldiers. Yet, until 1968, only about 22 percent of film shown on television covered actual battles. As in past wars, even this limited footage was partly censored by the military. Media still followed guidelines that discouraged using shots of wounded or dead American soldiers. "We had to file it [a story] with the intelligence officer for whatever unit you were with," said Cronkite. "Then that went to the army . . . [intelligence] officer, and he would pass it for

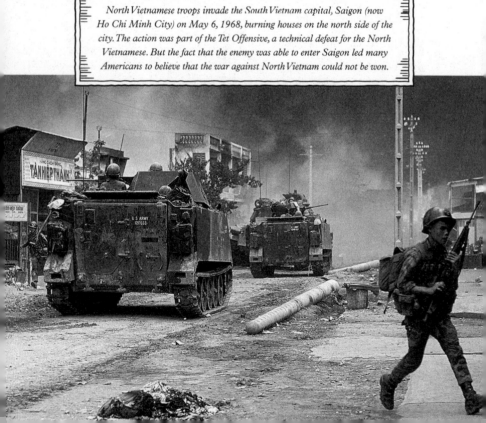

North Vietnamese troops invade the South Vietnam capital, Saigon (now Ho Chi Minh City) on May 6, 1968, burning houses on the north side of the city. The action was part of the Tet Offensive, a technical defeat for the North Vietnamese. But the fact that the enemy was able to enter Saigon led many Americans to believe that the war against North Vietnam could not be won.

transmission, or sometimes made deletions and changes . . . There were certain things we knew weren't going to pass. We tried to get by with them because we were trying to report everything we could. But casualties, for instance—they weren't anxious to let the enemy know how successful they had been in any given action, how many lives had been claimed."

The media changed its mostly positive view of American success in Vietnam after North Vietnam launched mass attacks on the South in late January 1968. Called the Tet Offensive (because it started on the first day of Tet, the Vietnamese New Year), the attacks focused on cities held by the South Vietnamese and American armies. News photographs and film footage captured North Vietnamese troops literally at the presidential palace, the airport, and even on the U.S. Embassy grounds in Saigon. It shocked Americans that the enemy could reach so far when they had mostly been told the United States and South Vietnam were winning.

NBC News reported on February 20 that "American Marines are so bogged down in Hue [a large South Vietnamese city] that nobody will even predict when the battle will end . . . More than 500 Marines have been wounded and 100 killed since the fighting in Hue began . . . Most of the city is now in rubble . . . and many Vietnamese say the fight isn't really worth it now that their city is dead."

The North Vietnamese were eventually forced to retreat, having lost tens of thousands of soldiers. Technically, this was a military

A NEWS MAN ON CENSORSHIP

Years after the Vietnam War, Walter Cronkite said that "they should have had censorship in Vietnam. I believe there should be censorship in wartime . . . I'm more comfortable when we are clear that our reporting is not putting our troops in jeopardy and . . . prolonging the killing."

But he also said, "Any war situation . . . is the most intimate commitment that the American government can make of its people. This is our war, our troops, our boys, our girls. We [the public] need to know every detail about how they are performing . . . both when they perform well and when they perform badly. It's more important when they perform badly . . . Correspondents should be there reporting on it . . . Their dispatches should go through a censorship procedure so that no military secrets are given to the enemy. But there is the report; it is there for history."

defeat for North Vietnam and a victory for the United States and South Vietnam. But to an American audience, the violent media images and the progress the North Vietnamese had been able to make did not add up to a victory. Toward the end of the Tet Offensive, Cronkite aired an hour-long special on CBS. "It seems now more certain than ever that the bloody experience of Vietnam is to end in a stalemate."

After the Tet Offensive, even government statements about Vietnam emphasized finding an acceptable peace plan rather than winning. Republican Richard Nixon campaigned for the presidency against Democrat Hubert Humphrey in 1968. One of his campaign brochures read: "Every American wants peace in Viet Nam." Nixon won the election and became president in 1969. He won reelection in 1972. His plan was to gradually withdraw American troops, at the same time building up the strength of South Vietnamese troops.

Despite his promise to turn responsibility over to the South Vietnamese, Nixon escalated the war. In April 1970, he bombed Cambodia, a neutral country next to Vietnam, and sent American soldiers there. North Vietnamese troops had taken refuge in Cambodia. He argued that this was a way to keep pressure on North Vietnam until South Vietnamese troops were ready to take over. Nixon kept the action a secret. After the press was allowed to report what was happening, many Americans protested the Cambodia invasion. There were demonstrations and campus shutdowns at colleges across the United States, and also criticism from Congress, and of course, the press itself. It wasn't until January 1973 that a peace treaty with North Vietnam was signed.

> *President Richard Nixon gives an outdoor press conference on March 12, 1971. Nixon famously disliked the news media. "Never forget," he told his advisors, "the press is the enemy."*

Nixon, famously, did not like the news media. "Never forget," he told two national security advisors only weeks after he was re-elected president in 1972, "the press is the enemy, the press is the enemy, the press is the enemy . . . Write that on a blackboard 100 times." In fact, Nixon had a good amount of positive press and public support. But he was angry at press that did not agree with him. He kept an "enemies list" that included many journalists. He planned ways to discredit them and make their lives more difficult. For example, he had the Internal Revenue Service question their tax returns or had the FBI illegally tap their phones to listen to their private conversations. Nixon's effort to use the courts to stop publication of a classified history of presidential policy in Vietnam led to one of the most important Supreme Court decisions concerning freedom of the press.

On June 13, 1971, the *New York Times* published an article under the headline: "Vietnam Archive: Pentagon Study Traces 3 Decades of Growing U.S. Involvement." This was an excerpt from a study of American participation in Vietnam, written in 1967. It showed that none of the presidents who were sending troops there believed that the United States could win the war. Yet, throughout the years of the Kennedy and Johnson administrations, the government had publicly claimed victory was possible with more American troops. These presidents did not want to be the first president in American history to lose a war.

The study was classified—it was not meant to be shown to the public. But Daniel Ellsberg, a military analyst for the government who had once supported the war, believed the public deserved to know the government had been lying. He secretly copied the study, even though it was classified "top secret." He gave it to reporters at the *New York Times*, the *Washington Post*, and other newspapers.

Was what Daniel Ellsberg did illegal? He had exposed a confidential government report. The Nixon government eventually charged him for violating the 1917 Espionage Act, the one passed during World War I. The act forbade "the unauthorized possession of . . . any document . . . relating to the national defense which information the possessor has reason to believe could be used to the injury of the United States." Ellsberg went to trial in 1973, but the charges were dropped. He was never found guilty and never went to prison.

Had the *New York Times* violated the law by publishing parts of a top secret study so that millions of people could see that the government had not told the truth? By the end of the same day of publication, the federal government demanded that the *Times* print no more of what became known as the Pentagon Papers.

The government asked a federal court in New York State for an injunction—a court order blocking further publication of the study. What the government ordered was prior restraint— forbidding publication before an article could be printed and made public. This was a form of censorship that was rarely used past the eighteenth century. The government argued that publishing the study would do great harm to the country's defense. The *Times'* lawyers said it gave no proof of what this harm would be.

After a federal judge ordered the New York Times *to cease publishing the Pentagon Papers, editor James Greenfield (left) and the newspaper's Washington bureau journalists Max Frankel (center) and Fred P. Graham (right) meet to discuss their next move.*

The judge ruled in the *Times'* favor. The government appealed the decision, which went to a higher New York State court. This court voted to uphold the ban on publishing. If the newspaper published the study, it would be breaking the law.

In the meantime, the *Washington Post* had published some of the Pentagon Papers. The government went to the federal court in Washington, D.C., to stop further publication. The court decided in the *Post*'s favor. Unlike the *New York Times* case, the federal appeals court in Washington, D.C., ruled that the *Post* could publish excerpts from the Pentagon Papers.

These decisions contradicted each other. In addition, the *Times* believed the injunction against them was unfair. Together, the two newspapers appealed to the Supreme Court for a final decision.

THE COURT RULES ON PRIOR RESTRAINT IN THE 1930S

In 1930, the Supreme Court was asked to decide the issue of whether prior restraint is legal, even though it had pretty much been eliminated as a government practice since the eighteenth century. Its decision in *Near v. Minnesota* set a precedent that prior restraint was illegal. Forty years later, it would help the judges make their decision about publishing the Pentagon Papers.

During the 1920s, Jay Near and Howard Guilford printed racist, hate-filled articles in the *Saturday Press* in Minneapolis. They accused government officials of working with criminals and taking bribes. Some of the accusations were based on truth. Guilford was shot, allegedly by gangsters. The Minneapolis chief of police responded by banning sale of the newspaper because it was "inciting to riot."

When the *Saturday Press* began to publish again, it ran anti-Semitic, anti-black, and anti-labor articles that were prejudiced and offensive. For example, "It is Jew thugs who have 'pulled' practically every robbery in the city," the paper wrote. In 1925, the county attorney used the Minnesota "gag" law against the *Press*. This called for stopping the publication of a "malicious, scandalous and defamatory newspaper, magazine or other periodical." Violation of the law was considered a nuisance that might lead to public disturbances.

The Minnesota state court ordered an injunction against the *Saturday Press*. It could not be published at all. Newspapers, even those with very different views from the *Press* that objected to the hateful language, said the injunction violated the First Amendment. *Chicago Tribune* publisher Robert McCormick called the law "tyrannical, despotic, un-American and oppressive."

When the case came before the Supreme Court, lawyers for Near argued that shutting down the paper to prevent publication was censorship, or prior restraint. They also pointed out that the articles published before the injunction had not led to any violence or public upset. The Supreme Court agreed. Chief Justice Charles Evans Hughes wrote the decision in 1931. He stated: "It is well understood . . . that it [the First Amendment] was intended to prevent all such *previous restraints* [censorship before printing] upon publications . . . The liberty of the press was to be unrestrained." The Minnesota law was found to be unconstitutional on the basis of the First Amendment.

Washington Post *reporters Carl Bernstein (*left*) and Bob Woodward (*right*) won the prestigious Pulitzer Prize for their investigative journalism uncovering the Watergate scandal. The scandal led to Richard Nixon's resignation as president. This photograph shows Woodward and Bernstein in the* Post's *newsroom on May 7, 1973.*

The case was named *New York Times Co. v. United States.* The newspapers won, with six judges voting to allow publication and three judges disagreeing.

Justice Hugo Black explained the Court's decision: "Only a free and unrestrained press can effectively expose deception in government. And paramount among the responsibilities of a free press is the duty to prevent any part of the government from deceiving the people and sending them off to distant lands to die of . . . foreign shot and shell . . . Far from deserving condemnation for their courageous reporting, the *New York Times,* the *Washington Post,* and other newspapers should be commended for serving the purpose that the Founding Fathers saw so clearly. In revealing the workings of government that led to the Viet Nam war, the newspapers nobly did precisely that which the Founders hoped and trusted they would do."

New York Times Co. v. United States was a big victory for freedom of the press. More excerpts from the Pentagon Papers were published over time. The Pentagon Papers gave a history of policy decisions, but they did not reveal military strategy. It is hard to tell how much impact their publication had on the conduct of the war. But many Americans were upset that the presidents and other officials of the United States had lied to them. Vietnam marked a change in both the media and the public's trust in government.

The press also helped put an end to Nixon's political career. Bob Woodward and Carl Bernstein, reporters for the *Washington Post*, conducted one of the most famous investigative journalism exposés of any president. In June 1972, they were assigned to write about a break-in by five burglars at offices in the Watergate building complex in Washington, D.C. One of these offices belonged to the Democratic National Committee. Based on extensive research and information from a secret source, the reporters eventually linked the break-in to Nixon, who was running for reelection as president. He had been hoping to learn something useful about the Democratic campaign. Nixon was reelected. But a series of articles in the *Post* revealing Nixon's role, and a book published by Woodward and Bernstein, *All the President's Men*, created a scandal that led to Nixon's resignation as president in 1974.

CHAPTER 6

FREEDOM FOR THE STUDENT PRESS

In December 1965, several students in Des Moines, Iowa, decided to wear black armbands to school to protest the war in Vietnam. When school officials found out, they announced that any student wearing an armband would have to take it off or be suspended. Thirteen-year-old Mary Beth Tinker wore the armband anyway, as did her sixteen-year-old brother, John; eleven-year-old sister, Hope; and eight-year-old brother, Paul. Sixteen-year-old Christopher Eckhardt also wore one. They were suspended. The students came back to school in January without the armbands but wore black clothes for the rest of the year. With their parents' help, they sued the school district, believing their right to free expression of beliefs under the First Amendment had been violated.

Both the federal district court and the federal court of appeals upheld the school district's decision. In 1968, the case went to the Supreme Court as *Tinker v. Des Moines Independent Community School District*. In 1969, the Court ruled 7–2 in favor of the

Mary Beth Tinker (right), her brother Paul (center), and their mother, Lorena Tinker (left), hear the news that the Supreme Court decided in their favor in Tinker v. Des Moines. *The Court's decision upheld the right of free expression for students. Mary Beth and Paul are wearing the black antiwar armbands for which they were suspended from school.*

students. "It can hardly be argued that either students or teachers shed their constitutional rights to freedom of speech or expression at the schoolhouse gate," wrote Justice Abe Fortas. "School officials do not possess absolute authority over their students. Students . . . are possessed of fundamental rights which the State must respect . . . They may not be confined to the expression of those sentiments that are officially approved." The only way punishing students for expressing their beliefs was valid, Fortas wrote, was if it "substantially interfere[d]" with the running of the school, or involved "substantial disorder or invasion of the rights of others." This is important in judging whether hate speech should be allowed in schools.

Tinker was not a case about press freedom for students. Nothing written was censored or punished. But press and speech are related, and both fall under the category of "expression," which can also include actions like the wearing of armbands. The Supreme Court's ruling in *Tinker* had an important influence on the way the law viewed a student's right to support or protest controversial opinions in public schools.

In 1988, however, a case involving a student newspaper, *Hazelwood School District v. Kuhlmeier*, modified that decision. The Supreme Court decided that students' rights to a free press can be limited by their school officials. The justices based their decision on their idea of community values; in this case, that articles in a school newspaper were inappropriate or offensive for younger high school students to read. Their decision was still influencing judgments as of this printing.

In May 1983, students in a journalism class at Hazelwood East High School, near St. Louis, Missouri, were putting out the last issue of the school newspaper for the year. They included articles on teenage pregnancy and on the way divorce affected kids. The first featured the stories of Hazelwood East girls who had become pregnant; their real names were not used. The second included

The Weekend Magazine of the St. Louis Globe-Democrat / Feb. 9, 1985

GLOBE
W E E D

RICHARD "ONION" HORTON IS STILL MAD AT THE WORLD
St. Louis' most outspoken black commentator says he'll never change until America does. And, by the way, why is he called Onion?

Too hot for Hazelwood

These three young women decided to make a federal case out of it when officials of Hazelwood East High School deleted four articles — dealing with teenage pregnancy, teenage marriage, runaways and the effects of divorce on children — from their student newspaper. The stories were deemed "not appropriate," or "too sensitive," according to court testimony. We thought you'd like to read all about it. So we are publishing the stories for the first time.

Cathy Kuhlmeier (left), Leanne Tippett (center), and Leslie Smart (right) challenged their high school principal's decision to censor articles in their student newspaper. They are shown here two years later in an edition of St. Louis Globe, *which printed the censored articles. In* Hazelwood School District v. Kuhlmeier, *the Supreme Court decided that school officials could censor material they thought inappropriate for students.*

comments from a student who felt her father was to blame for the divorce. The faculty advisor who taught the journalism class approved the articles.

The school's principal, however, had the final say over what could be published. He believed the subjects were not suitable for younger students. He thought that readers would recognize the pregnant girls even though their names were changed. He also thought that parents mentioned in the divorce article should have a chance to object to its publication. The principal censored two pages of the issue, including the articles covering pregnancy and divorce. He did not let the journalism students know of his decision.

The school newspaper layout editor, Cathy Kuhlmeier, a junior when the articles were censored, and reporters Leslie Smart, also a junior, and Leanne Tippett, a senior, sued school officials. They were helped by a lawyer from the American Civil Liberties Union (ACLU). They claimed that censoring the articles violated their First Amendment right of freedom of the press. The federal court in eastern Missouri ruled against the students. But when the case went to the Missouri appeals court, it reversed this decision, saying that the students' rights had been violated.

This time the school district, rather than the press, challenged the decision. The case, *Hazelwood School District v. Kuhlmeier*, went to the Supreme Court. On January 13, 1988, it decided in favor of the school district. "A school must be able to set high standards for the student speech that is disseminated under its auspices—standards that may be higher than those demanded by some newspaper publishers . . . in the 'real' world—and may refuse to disseminate student speech that does not meet those standards," wrote Justice Byron White.

"In addition, a school must be able to take into account the emotional maturity of the intended audience . . . A school must also retain the authority to refuse to sponsor student speech that might reasonably be perceived to advocate drug or alcohol use, irresponsible sex, or conduct otherwise inconsistent with 'the shared values' of a civilized social order." White continued, "We hold that educators do not offend the First Amendment by exercising editorial control over the style and content of student speech in school-sponsored expressive activities so long as their actions are reasonably related to legitimate pedagogical [teaching] concerns."

The Supreme Court's decision in *Hazelwood* was the opposite of the decision in *Tinker*. Three justices disagreed with the majority. "The young men and women of Hazelwood East expected a civics lesson, but not the one the Court teaches them today," wrote Justice William Brennan. "Such unthinking contempt for individual rights is intolerable from any state official. It is particularly insidious from [a school principal] to whom the public entrusts the task of inculcating in its youth an appreciation for the cherished democratic liberties that our constitution guarantees."

As this book goes to press, *Hazelwood School District v. Kuhlmeier* is the most recent Supreme Court decision regarding freedom of the press for school newspapers. The Court took the role of a parent in deciding what is appropriate for teenagers to read. It did make a distinction between a newspaper that was part of an actual class and one operated independently of the school by students. But overall it has had what is called a "chilling"

TODAY'S STUDENT EDITORS BELIEVE IN FREEDOM OF THE PRESS

"I believe that freedom of the press is one of the most important parts of a democracy. Not only does most of the country's population depend on the press for our daily information, but we rely on it because it goes back to the original values that the Founders laid out in the Constitution . . . The press protects us, whether the information it states is harmful or hard to hear. It's our main information source and protects us from an overbearing government. Without it, we couldn't express our true opinions as journalists and we would not be as aware of our surroundings."

–Sienna E., senior, California

"The media occupies an extremely unique position as an informant to the public, a forum for discussion, and a referendum on the actions of our citizens. I can't imagine democracy without any of those components."

–Kelly A., senior, Washington, D.C.

"I don't believe that the free speech of anyone should be limited if it is not inciting to violence or hate, especially for young people in a format like a school newspaper. Limiting these freedoms for young people in particular would only have damaging results. If we don't care about press freedoms for young people, those young people will grow up and not understand the importance of journalism and reporting as adults. And with the current climate around the president, 'fake news' and otherwise, this generation's attitude towards . . . press freedoms is especially crucial."

–Arthur K., sophomore, Wisconsin

effect—school officials considering articles will be more likely to censor anything that makes them uncomfortable, rather than rely on the First Amendment.

Since the Hazelwood decision, the Student Press Law Center and other civil rights organizations have promoted the passing of state laws to protect press freedom for high school students. By early 2020, thirteen states had passed such laws and one was pending in New York.

Student journalists today still have to decide to print what they feel is important, especially if it is controversial. "I think there are definitely . . . expectations of what a young child should be reading versus an adult," explained Sienna E., a senior and editor of her school newspaper in California. "Hazelwood . . . set a precedent . . . that kids need to be protected from the seemingly 'bad' topics. But I feel that every student can make a choice for themselves, and they can't be protected from the more serious topics forever."

"Nobody should ever be restricted in their reading choices, particularly in the context of secondary education," said Kelly A., a senior and an editor of his student newspaper in Washington, D.C. "Anyone who says otherwise doesn't realize that younger kids (especially younger high school students) are already exposed to content made for more 'mature' audiences on a daily basis."

Kelly was able to work with school officials when, "in November 2018, there was an incident on campus where two seniors were suspended for using anti-Semitic language. The editors . . . wanted

Student journalists from New York State listen to state senator Brian Kavanaugh and assemblywoman Donna Lupardo (far right) talk about their support of the Student Journalist Free Speech Act. The act would protect students' First Amendment rights.

to publish a story about what had happened because we saw the incident as an important moment for the . . . community to learn from and discuss. Several members of the administration were vehemently opposed to running the story, but after meeting with them and our faculty advisor, we reached a compromise that allowed us to publish the story." Kelly's newspaper has also published stories on "violations of academic integrity and party culture. Both topics are . . . incredibly relevant in the lives of . . . students, but seldom discussed in a public forum."

In 2018–2019, Arthur K., a sophomore, was a news editor for a student newspaper in Wisconsin. "Earlier in this school year," he said, "it was reported that the immigration agency, ICE [U.S. Immigration and Customs Enforcement], had come to [a school in our district] looking to take someone into custody . . . It didn't seem as though there were many answers as to what had happened, so for my first article for our school newspaper, I interviewed . . . School Resource Officers . . . and then talked to some of the people in the district who . . . work with undocumented students about what they felt and were experiencing. We all agreed that this was an important story for students, staff, and the community at large to be informed about, since immigration policy and what happens to undocumented immigrants is a big national issue right now."

In addition to straight news and feature stories, student newspapers feature editorial comments that at best give a context for what is being reported. Alissandre C., a senior and editor of her school newspaper in California, was "involved in the editorials . . . which are based on the most controversial/deepest story of each issue . . . The more controversial our topics are, the more we feel we need to use our platform and spread awareness about them. We've never turned down a topic. Some . . . examples are vaping [use of electronic cigarettes] and misgendering." In April 2019, Alissandre's newspaper published a story on elementary school children with severe food allergies who are bullied by other students for being different.

In 2017, Jahnavi Dave, then an eighth grader from Virginia, won a *Washington Post* essay contest for kids about World Press Freedom Day. "We may not know it," she wrote, "but history is being made right now, in this moment. From the change in power in government domestically, to the growing terror internationally, to the climate crisis being faced globally, we are part of an ever-changing society. As citizens and residents of the United States of America, it is important to be informed about everything going on around us. Without having knowledge about current problems, we cannot work together to solve them . . . Now more than ever, it is important for the free press to portray the world without any filters."

CHAPTER 7

National Security, 9/11, and Press Censorship

B y the end of the 1980s, the United States was again at war. The Persian Gulf War (1990–1991) once again changed the relationship of the government to the press. In August 1990, Iraq, led by Saddam Hussein, invaded Kuwait and eventually claimed it as part of their country. The United Nations condemned the action. In January 1991, the United States, under President George H. W. Bush, led an international force in an air attack against Iraq. In little more than a month, the war was over. Kuwait was freed, but Hussein remained in power.

Unlike the Vietnam War, when the press had relative freedom to move about the war zone, during the Gulf War journalists were organized into groups or "pools." Each pool included print and radio reporters and television cameramen from different newspapers and broadcast stations. Public affairs officers under the military command accompanied them to chosen sites. Images for television and print media came from cameras attached to American bomber airplanes, which captured video

U.S. Marines disembark from a helicopter and spread out over the desert as part of Operation Desert Shield during the Persian Gulf War (also known as the First Iraq War). During the war, journalists were grouped into "pools" and accompanied to chosen sites by the military.

feed. Shots of bombing showed dramatic streaks of light in the sky but did not show the destruction on the ground. Most of the press's information came from daily briefings by the military. Since the government, represented by military personnel, strictly controlled what the press was hearing and seeing, there was little need for censorship. The news media presented to Americans what the Bush administration wanted them to know.

The media reflected the government's assertions that "smart" bombs—those guided by lasers that could precisely strike a military target—protected Iraqi civilians from harm. An American watching the nightly news might think that no schools, houses, or mosques (most Iraqis practice Islam) were hit. As it came out later, however, most of the bombs used were not "smart" bombs and many missed their targets. Roads, railroads, utilities like electricity, and factories were routinely hit, all affecting daily life.

After the war ended, Pete Williams, assistant secretary of defense for public affairs, claimed "the press gave the American people the best war coverage they ever had." But many journalists and historians now disagree with that, saying the pool system kept them from reporting on immediate or negative aspects of the war. With the information they were given, the press often compared the war to a video game. Human pilots did not transport the "smart" bombs to their targets but controlled them electronically—and safely—from a distance. Most of the briefings given to pool reporters came from military public information officers, who, according to journalist Christiane Amanpour, were "concerned 95 percent with image . . . Increasingly, the balance is too much in favor of controlling image and not security."

The Persian Gulf War also signaled a change in the way Americans received news reports. The Cable News Network (CNN) had a broadcaster in Iraq when the bombing began on January 17. CNN provided twenty-four-hour coverage. Although it reported from inside a hotel in Baghdad, Iraq's capital, and not in the field, the fact that it could deliver the news available at any time, night or day, made the station extremely popular. Today, the internet supplies twenty-four-hour coverage from innumerable sources, but in 1991, it was an innovation.

INSTANT NEWS ON THE INTERNET

Print and broadcast media started posting news websites in the 1990s. But the development of the internet goes back to the early 1960s, when scientists were researching how computers might "talk" to each other—that is, be linked up to share information. Their projects were supported by the Defense Advanced Research Projects Agency (DARPA), a government organization with links to many universities. DARPA was concerned with new technology that would help the military. In 1969, computers at Stanford University and the University of California at Los Angeles were connected to communicate with each other for the first time. Scientific researchers around the world were strongly interested in creating a system that would allow them to quickly access each other's information. The first group of internet users was scientists at universities.

But the technology soon spread to other uses. In 1971, the first email was developed. In 1977, three commercial models of PCs (personal computers) were released. The same year, the PC modem was invented, which connected a computer to a wire that transmitted the requested information, something like the way a telephone works. British scientist Tim Berners-Lee proposed the World Wide Web in 1989 and wrote the code for it in 1990. A year later, the first web page appeared. The search engine Google began operating in 1998.

As more and more people turned to the internet for information and entertainment, print and broadcast news media lost some of their audiences. CNN, the *Chicago Tribune*, and the Raleigh, North Carolina, *News & Observer*

were among the first to offer online news sites in the early to mid-1990s. The *News & Observer* soon became a go-to place for sports fans when it specialized in posting scores as soon as games were finished. A fan did not have to wait for the morning newspaper to learn the results. Most newspapers now have online as well as print editions, and radio and television stations also have websites. Some newspapers are no longer in print at all but only online. The *Seattle Post-Intelligencer* was one of the first newspapers to convert, in 2009, after nearly 150 years in print.

The rise of social media in the early twenty-first century also changed the way people could receive news and opinions. Facebook went online in 2004, although at first it was only meant to connect college students with each other. YouTube appeared in 2005 and Twitter in 2006. Pinterest and Instagram, which allow images to be shared, launched in 2010. Newspapers and broadcast media now have their own Facebook, Twitter, and YouTube accounts.

The first blog was said to have been posted in 1994; now independent bloggers, who are often not professional journalists, are a huge presence on the internet. Bloggers offer their own editorial opinions, competing with traditional media for audiences. In a 2017 survey, 43 percent of Americans reported that they got their news online, closing in on the number who get their news from watching television. An even smaller percentage of Americans mainly get their news from print media.

This digital map shows how cities around the world are connected by the internet.

Smoke pours from the top of one of the World Trade Center buildings after it is hit by terrorists who hijacked an American plane on September 11, 2001. Soon after, another plane crashed into the second Trade Center building and both were destroyed.

Television and internet sites were able to report continuously in 2001, when an attack took place that has affected the government's view of national security ever since. On September 11, 2001, an American plane hijacked by terrorists struck the north tower of the World Trade Center in New York City. Eighteen minutes later, a second plane, also hijacked, struck the south tower. An hour later, both towers collapsed. In the meantime, another hijacked plane hit the side of the Pentagon, near Washington, D.C. A fourth plane crashed in Pennsylvania, killing everyone aboard. Almost three thousand people were killed that day, including firefighters and police who rushed to the rescue. Millions of Americans saw the Trade Center towers collapse as it happened, and that image would be broadcast again and again.

American newspapers overwhelmingly responded to the attacks on the World Trade Center as an "Act of War," as the headline in the *New York Post* read on September 12. *USA Today* used the same headline, with the subhead, "Terrorists Strike, Death Toll 'Horrendous.'" "U.S. Attacked," read the *New York Times*, which called the buildings' destruction and the death toll "a creeping horror." The *Atlanta Constitution*'s headline was simply "Outrage." The *Detroit Free Press* called September 11 "America's Darkest Day." The New York *Daily News* declared bluntly, "It's War."

Al-Qaeda, an Islamic extremist organization headed by Osama bin Laden, was responsible for the attacks. Al-Qaeda objected to the American military presence in Saudi Arabia and other parts of the Middle East and the American support of Israel. Bin Laden and some of his followers were based in Afghanistan, supported by the Taliban, an extremely conservative Islamic political and religious group that had taken over control of the country. Soon, the United States would be at war there.

In September, American media were ready to back any aggressive response the government took to the destruction. "Nine-eleven," as it came to be called, would turn out to be the single most critical event to date to affect the relationship between the government and the press in the twenty-first century. Since September 11, 2001, the United States has been engaged in a war on terrorism that extends beyond national boundaries and does not depend on actual occurrences in the country. The charge of violating national security can be used against any journalistic report if the president decides to use it. Presidential communications and intelligence agencies like the CIA and the FBI have become more secretive, not always letting the press know what they are doing, especially as it relates to the constitutional rights of American citizens.

 ## A NOTABLE RESPONSE TO TERRORISM

A leader's statements can affect the mood and actions of Americans. They can be aggressive or calm. A week after 9/11, President George W. Bush visited the Islamic Center of Washington, D.C., where he called on Americans not to threaten or act violently toward millions of Muslims who were American citizens. "The face of terror is not the true faith of Islam," he said. "That's not what Islam is all about. Islam is peace . . . It is my honor to be meeting with [Islamic] leaders who feel just the same way I do. They're outraged, they're sad. They love America just as much as I do."

President George W. Bush speaks at the Islamic Center of Washington, D.C.,
on September 17, 2001, a week after the destruction of the World Trade Center.
He called for no violence against American Muslims who, though
not connected with the terrorist acts, were facing prejudice and hostility.

U.S. helicopters fire their guns in a training exercise in Afghanistan on October 4, 2009. The United States went to war in Afghanistan in 2001 to search out Osama bin Laden, who had orchestrated the 9/11 attacks. At the time this book went to press, the country was still involved in military action in Afghanistan.

The United States and Britain began an air-bombing campaign in Afghanistan in October 2001. The American press supported this action. "The media have really flown the flag, acted as patriots, been front and center in presenting themselves as behind the war effort," said Robert Lichter of the Center for Media and Public Affairs in an article in the *Los Angeles Times* on November 18, 2001.

Two years later, Defense Secretary Donald Rumsfeld declared to reporters in Afghanistan on May 1, 2003, that "major combat" in the country had ended. But American forces have stayed in Afghanistan in greater or lesser numbers through the presidencies of Bush, Barack Obama, and Donald Trump. The Taliban revived its power in 2005, and various Afghan governments and military forces have been too weak to unite the country.

Unlike Afghanistan, Iraq had not been overtly involved in the 9/11 attacks, although President Bush asserted that the country supported terrorists. It was thought that Saddam Hussein was working on developing and storing nuclear, biological, and chemical weapons. These are called weapons of mass destruction (WMDs).

For months, the Republican Bush administration hammered home the idea that Iraq possessed WMDs. "Our intelligence officials estimate that Saddam Hussein had the materials to produce as much as 500 tons of . . . nerve agent," Bush said on January 28, 2003. Democrats largely agreed. They overwhelmingly voted for a bipartisan congressional resolution authorizing war that stated: "Iraq . . . poses a continuing threat to the national security of the United States, . . . continuing to possess and develop a significant chemical and biological weapons capability."

Many news outlets printed and broadcast these accusations, without objection, before and on the eve of the war. Soon after the air strikes started, the *New York Times* backed up the Bush administration's claim that an important reason to go to war was to find weapons of mass destruction. In a front-page story on April 21, it reported that "a scientist who claims to have worked in Iraq's chemical weapons program for more than a decade has told the American military team that Iraq destroyed chemical weapons and biological warfare equipment only days before the war began . . ." The story said the unnamed scientist had taken Americans to see a "supply of materials that proved to be the building blocks of illegal weapons." The *Times* has national influence and sends its stories by wire service to newspapers around the world. Soon after this article appeared, the *Rocky Mountain News* in Denver, declared, "Scientist Says Iraq Retained Illicit Weapons," while the *Seattle Post-Intelligencer* stated, "Outlawed Arsenals Destroyed by the Iraqis Before the War." These claims were shown to be false, but not before they reached Americans across the country.

In February 2004, President George W. Bush (center, at podium) names Chuck Robb (left) and Laurence Silberman (right) to investigate how accurate intelligence reports were that claimed that Iraq had weapons of mass destruction. The United States went to war with Iraq over this claim. No weapons of mass destruction were found.

Even the uncritical mainstream American media began to question the reasons the United States went to war in the spring of 2003. For one thing, the WMDs were not discovered then and they never have been. Hussein, target of the attacks, was not captured and executed until 2006. "It is not our job to be cheerleaders," said Sandra Mims Rowe, editor of the Portland *Oregonian*. "Information about this war is so filtered that I'm less concerned about our giving away military secrets than I am with whether we're asking tough enough questions . . . [and] being suspicious of pat answers and evasions."

During the Iraq War, however, the American military gave the news media an opportunity it had not had in previous wars. Some reporters and photographers were embedded—placed—in military units. They were allowed to go with these units into combat zones. There were about six hundred journalists embedded with American forces during the Iraq invasion. Embedding was the result of the press's demand for greater access to battle zones. It had the advantage of providing safety to journalists traveling to dangerous areas and of letting them directly observe and write about combat.

Washington Post editor and columnist David Ignatius was embedded with U.S. military in Iraq and Afghanistan. He appreciated the chance to see what was happening in a war zone. "But embedding comes with a price," he wrote in 2010. "We are observing these wars from just one perspective [the American military], not seeing them whole. When you see my byline . . . you should not think that I am out among ordinary people, asking questions of all sides. I am usually inside an American military bubble. That vantage point has value, but it is hardly a full picture."

Embedded journalists are able to give the government's point of view. In return for one kind of access, they give up searching out different sources of information. This goes against the Founding Fathers' desire for the First Amendment to protect the press so that it can be a watchdog revealing controversial public actions. But, like Daniel Ellsberg when he released the Pentagon Papers to the print media in 1971, there are still whistle-blowers and newspapers ready to print their revelations. They can, like Ellsberg, be people who have worked for the government but feel that constitutional rights are being violated and that the public has a right to know. The whistle-blowers are likely to be prosecuted by the government, tried in court, and given jail sentences. Journalists can face pressure to reveal who gave them the information.

Judith Miller, then a reporter for the *New York Times*, spent eighty-five days in jail in 2005 for refusing to reveal her source for an article that uncovered the identity of an American spy. She was held in "contempt of court" for not giving evidence to the grand jury hearing the case. Matthew Cooper, a reporter for *Time* magazine, was also held in contempt but avoided jail time when his source gave permission for him to reveal his identity. But an American journalist actually going to prison is unusual.

James Risen, another *New York Times* reporter, was called before the court twice to reveal his relationship with Jeffrey Sterling.

Journalists are briefed by U.S. Marine colonel Ronald Bailey (right) as they get ready to cover the Iraq War. During the war, journalists were "embedded" with American troops and could accompany them into combat zones.

Sterling, a former CIA officer, was accused of giving classified information to Risen for his book on the CIA and the Bush administration, published in 2006. Risen was pressured until 2015, when the government finally decided not to call him to testify. Sterling was convicted anyway on evidence of phone records and emails that showed he had been in contact with the reporter. Although it came to nothing, the legal pursuit of Risen alarmed journalists.

In 2010, WikiLeaks, a whistle-blowing media organization, published classified and "sensitive" documents about the wars in Afghanistan and Iraq. Chelsea Manning (then Bradley Manning), a United States soldier and intelligence analyst in Iraq, provided some 480,000 army reports, including statistics on unreported civilian deaths, a number higher than the American military had reported. Julian Assange, who founded WikiLeaks, lived outside

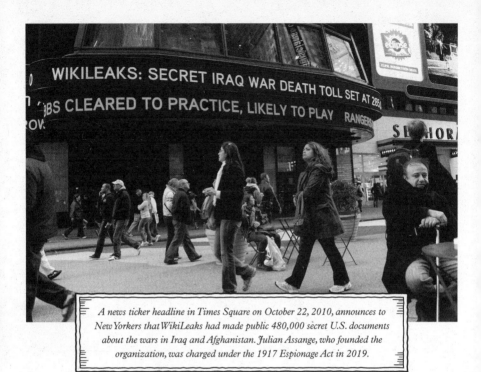

A news ticker headline in Times Square on October 22, 2010, announces to New Yorkers that WikiLeaks had made public 480,000 secret U.S. documents about the wars in Iraq and Afghanistan. Julian Assange, who founded the organization, was charged under the 1917 Espionage Act in 2019.

the United States after Manning's information was published. Although Assange was in prison in Britain in 2019, the United States government charged him on eighteen counts of violating the 1917 Espionage Act. They included publishing the information leaked by Manning.

"The charges . . . raised the difficult question of how—or whether—to distinguish WikiLeaks from journalists who frequently publish information the government would rather keep secret," wrote *USA Today* on May 23, 2019. Assange maintained he is not a journalist. The government agreed, arguing that he is no journalist and therefore not protected by the freedom of the press clause. But much of the press feels that prosecuting Assange sets a bad precedent. "Any government use of the Espionage Act to criminalize the . . . publication of classified information poses a dire threat to journalists seeking to publish such information in the public interest," believes Bruce Brown, executive director of the Reporters Committee for Freedom of the Press.

During Barack Obama's presidency (2009–2017), more whistleblowers—eight people—were charged than in all the other presidencies before him. But none of the reporters and newspapers who used the material they leaked went to court. Edward Snowden made headlines in 2013 when he leaked information from the National Security Agency (NSA), where he had worked as a government contractor. The documents revealed that the NSA carried out massive surveillance of the American public on internet and phone lines. The surveillance violated the privacy, and arguably the civil rights, of vast numbers of people who had done nothing illegal. Snowden did not hide his identity. He released the information to several newspapers, but left the United States before the information was published. He faces charges under the Espionage Act if he returns to this country. No journalist had to be asked to name him as a source.

When the government holds back information—especially when that information is revealed by whistleblowers—it can increase public suspicion that Americans are not learning the truth. Since 1967, journalists and ordinary citizens alike have been able to request government documents through various agencies under the Freedom of Information Act. There are exceptions that include classified information on national defense and foreign policy. After 9/11, when national security became a top priority George W. Bush's presidency was marked by secrecy. Barack

Obama promised that his administration would be more open, when he came to office in 2009. Yet journalists complained that the Obama administration did not force agencies to give out information as requirred under the Freedom of Information Act. These agencies can be understaffed and reluctant to deliver material that they believe might affect national security. Even when they do release information, it is often not in a timely manner, taking months or even years. In 2016, Obama signed into law the Freedom of Information Improvement Act, designed to aid access to government documents and records. However, it is still an imperfect system.

For the last forty years or so, presidents have answered reporters' questions at solo press conferences, which last about an hour. Journalists in the White House press corps met with the president to hear what he had to say about policy and current events. Bill Clinton held fifteen press conferences in his first year and a half as president, and George H. W. Bush held twenty-four. In the same time frame, Obama held six and Donald Trump held one. But as presidents give fewer and fewer formal press conferences, they still talk to the press in spontaneous, short question-and-answer sessions.

However, for Obama and Trump, there was less need to get the word out through the traditional press because of the internet. The White House maintains its own online news report. Obama's was the first administration to have in-house video reporting, producing *West Wing Week*, shown every Friday on the White House website. Obama also made use of the White House Facebook page.

Twitter, founded in 2006, was available to George W. Bush

President Barack Obama (far left, seated) briefs reporters in the Oval Office of the White House on December 3, 2015. Although presidents have given fewer and fewer formal press conferences in the last decades, they still talk to reporters in shorter, more informal sessions.

and Obama, but no president has relied on Twitter to directly reach Americans as much as President Trump. With Twitter, he can bypass the usual way presidential statements have been voiced. In his first 465 days in office, Trump tweeted 3,201 times, about seven times a day on average. These tweets proclaimed his successes, criticized his opponents, defended against attacks, and, often, took aim at the press. His continuous charges of "fake news" and portrayals of journalists he disagrees with as "enemies of the people" have discredited the press in the eyes of some Americans and outraged others. This has raised the questions, how important is the principle of freedom of the press and how much can it be damaged?

FAKE NEWS, REAL LIES, AND THE PRESS

I n 1835, the New York *Sun* reported that men were living on
the moon. These were not ordinary men. "They averaged
four feet in height, were covered, except on the face, with
short and glossy copper-colored hair, and had wings" like a bat's.
Unicorns also roamed the moon. So did a strange kind of beaver
that walked upright on two legs. The *Sun* explained that Sir John
Herschel, a respected astronomer, had made this discovery "by
means of a telescope of vast dimensions" that gave him "a distinct
view of objects in the moon . . . at the distance of a hundred yards."
The newspaper supposedly had taken the story from an article
published in the prestigious British *Journal of Science*.

The *Sun* described Herschel's findings in a series of six articles.
Each day, New Yorkers rushed to buy the paper to read the next
installment. Every other newspaper in the city ran its own articles.
They confirmed the story or argued and wondered about whether
it could be true. Herschel was real. He lived in South Africa and
had made important discoveries. But after the sixth article came

A lithograph in the New York Sun *published on August 28, 1835, illustrates the newspaper's claim that life had been discovered on the moon. The humans shown had wings like bats.*

out, a rival newspaper finally proclaimed that the moon story was a hoax—a trick. The *Sun* did not deny it.

Did the *Sun* go out of business for presenting a made-up story as factual? No. In fact, its readership increased. New Yorkers were delighted by the moon story. If they had believed it, it was thrilling to imagine. If they did not believe it, they enjoyed the deception. Newspapers up until the 1830s had been mainly supported by political parties. They were partisan and critical. The *Sun* represented a new kind of newspaper. It sold for a few pennies, was supported by advertising, and appealed to a large audience. The penny press, as it was called, did not go after factual news. It featured stories and jokes. Its readers wanted less information and more entertainment.

The *Sun*'s moon story is an actual example of fake news: the paper's editor knew it was false when he published it but wanted

ST. LOUIS POST-DISPATCH **NIGHT** EDITION FINANCIAL MARKETS SPORTS

Only Evening Paper in St. Louis With the Associated Press Night Service

"TITANIC" IS SINKING; PASSENGERS SAVED
Wireless Brought Aid After Giant Liner Hit Iceberg at Night Off Newfoundland

"FAKE" NEWS.

There Are a Lot of Unconscionable
Rascals in Journalistic Circles,

Making It Sometimes Difficult to Ascertain
True Facts.

> *A headline in the* St. Louis Post-Dispatch
> *announces that the passengers on the* Titanic *were
> saved. The newspaper appeared on April 15, 1912,
> the day before the enormous loss of life was known.
> Early reports like this can be false or misleading.*

> *"Fake News" is not new to
> the twenty-first century. Here
> the* Cincinnati Commercial
> Tribune *expresses concern
> about the phenomenon in 1890.*

readers to believe it was true. It was not a mistake. Fake news
intends to lie. It is not a new phenomenon of the twenty-first
century or here because of the internet. Benjamin Franklin printed
fake news that claimed the British were paying Native Americans
to kill women and children in the rebelling colonies. The stories
were meant to be as scary and sensational as possible to arouse
readers' emotions. Franklin wanted to provoke anger at the
British and loyalty from the colonists. Although fake news can
induce both fear and patriotism, it has been traditionally used
to sell newspapers—and now, to draw more readers to postings
on websites. Exciting and colorful stories do that.

In a world dominated by the internet and social media outlets
like Facebook, Instagram, YouTube, and Twitter, it is easier than
ever to willingly—or accidentally—spread fake news. In the past,
fake news came from established newspapers, such as the yellow
journalist publications the *New York World* and the *New York
Journal*. Now, online, fake news tends to come from highly
partisan political groups.

In today's media environment, "the capacity to disseminate [spread] misinformation, wild conspiracy theories, to paint the opposition in wildly negative light without any rebuttal—that has accelerated in ways that . . . make it very difficult to have a common conversation," Barack Obama said in an interview after the 2016 election.

During the 2016 presidential campaign between Democrat Hillary Clinton and Republican Donald Trump, fake news, deliberately placed, filled social media. Paul Horner ran several

Presidential candidates Donald Trump (left) and Hillary Clinton (right) debate each other on October 9, 2016, in St. Louis, Missouri.

fake websites, including one that declared that Clinton supporters had been paid $3,500 each to protest at Trump rallies. Horner later told the *Washington Post* he meant it as a hoax. But the story took off, and even Trump himself repeated it. Clinton was accused in fake news of selling weapons to ISIS, a militant terrorist group.

Also, during the 2016 campaign, Christopher Blair launched a page on Facebook as a joke. He called it "America's Last Line of Defense." It was meant to amuse liberal Democrats by creating phony stories that were extremely unlikely, even ridiculous. The website continued after the campaign. Blair has a large following of Trump supporters and other conservatives who believe and share the fake stories he posts. He has published stories that say California is going to switch to Muslim law, that illegal immigrants damaged the faces of the presidents on Mount Rushmore, and that Obama avoided the draft when he was nine years old. The site says in several places that the "news" is fake. One sentence reads "Nothing on this page is real." Yet his posts continue to go viral. He confirms what people already believe, so they take it to be the truth. And every time a post goes viral, he earns more money from ads posted with his stories.

There is a difference between deliberate (real) fake news that is meant to be funny, or a satire, or that is knowingly false because the author wants to excite the audience's emotions, and news that is honest but called fake because the person making the accusation doesn't like what he or she is reading or seeing. On February 6, 2017, President Trump tweeted, "Any negative

polls are fake news." He meant any polls that did not support his opinions or policies. On February 17, he called the major television networks, like ABC and CNN, as well as the *New York Times*, "the FAKE NEWS media." President Trump has also targeted other news media outlets, including MSNBC and the *Washington Post*. During his first two years in office, he rarely criticized the Fox News Channel, which regularly supported and even advanced his positions.

But Fox News host Christopher Wallace did ask hard questions of Trump when he interviewed him on November 18, 2018. "In 2017 . . . you tweeted this . . . 'The fake news media is not my enemy.

It is the enemy of the American people,'" said Wallace. "That's true, 100 percent," Trump replied. "No president has liked his press coverage," continued Wallace. "John Kennedy . . . canceled the subscription to the *New York Herald Tribune*. Nobody called it the enemy of the American people." Trump: "I'm calling the fake news is the enemy—it's fake, it's phony." Wallace: "But a lot of times, sir, it's just news you don't like." Wallace added, "Leaders in authoritarian countries like Russia, China, Venezuela, now repress the media using your words." Trump: "I can't talk for other people. I can only talk for me." Wallace: "But you're seen around the world as a beacon for repression."

On July 24, 2018, President Trump further attacked the news media, during a speech before a Veterans of Foreign Wars (VFW) convention. The VFW is an organization of people who have served in any U.S. war. During the speech, members of the press sat together in a special section at the back. "Don't believe the crap you see from these people—the fake news," Trump said, pointing to the press. The White House website noted this comment was followed by "applause." "And just remember," Trump later added. "What you're seeing and what you're reading is not what's happening."

VFW leaders quickly tweeted, "Today, we were disappointed to hear some of our members boo the press during President Trump's remarks. We rely on the media to spread the VFW message, and @CNN, @NBCNews, @ABC, @FoxNews, @CBSNews, & others on site today, were our invited guests. We were happy to have them there."

Frank Holeman (left), a correspondent for the New York Daily News, interviews American soldiers during the Korean War. American journalists have risked their lives in combat zones to report events as early as the Civil War. While they may disagree with some military and policy decisions, they have shown a wide sympathy for portraying the lives and dangers faced by ordinary soldiers.

"Like so many of my colleagues, I have covered this nation's wars for decades, working side by side with our soldiers, sailors, Marines and airmen," wrote Martha Raddatz, a journalist for ABC News. Raddatz said in an op-ed piece that she spent her career "[sharing] foxholes and flight decks with these brave Americans . . . Have those veterans who booed and taunted the media in response to Trump's cue forgotten that some members of the press corps are combat veterans? . . . Have they forgotten that since the wars in Afghanistan and Iraq began, hundreds of journalists have given their lives for their work, many times while reporting from U.S. war zones?"

Four days after Raddatz's op-ed piece appeared, President Trump tweeted, "I just cannot state strongly enough how totally dishonest much of the Media is. Truth doesn't matter to them, they only have their hatred & agenda . . . Enemy of the People!"

It is a big step to go from criticizing the press to calling the news media the "Enemy of the People." "The Fake News hates me saying that they are the Enemy of the People only because they know it's TRUE," Trump tweeted on August 5, 2018. "I am providing a great service by explaining this to the American People. They purposely cause great division & distrust. They can also cause War! They are very dangerous & sick." It is true that the press may influence the public's decision to support a war, but only Congress can declare one. Viewing the press as an "enemy," however, can make journalists themselves potential targets of violence. In fact, it makes committing violence toward reporters an acceptable thing to do.

In August 2017, a right-wing group posted a cartoon on Twitter showing a train labeled "Trump" killing a reporter from CNN. The cartoon's label read "Fake News Can't Stop the Trump Train." President Trump himself retweeted the cartoon. He did not criticize it.

This cartoon of the "Trump Train" running over a CNN reporter was posted on Twitter in August 2017. A half hour after Trump retweeted the cartoon, the White House deleted it from the president's Twitter stream. The cropped-off part on top says "Fake News Can't Stop the Trump Train."

On October 18, 2018, at a campaign rally for Representative Greg Gianforte of Montana, Trump praised him because Gianforte had physically assaulted a newspaper reporter the year before. "Any guy that can do a body slam—he's my kind of—he's my guy," Trump said. "He's a great guy, tough cookie." Gianforte had actually broken the law. He had to pay a fine and complete forty hours of community service and twenty hours of anger management counseling. Gianforte also donated $50,000 to the Committee to Protect Journalists.

More than criticize, President Trump has suggested concrete actions to limit press freedom. "Why do we work so hard in working with the media when it is corrupt? Take away credentials?" Trump tweeted on May 9, 2018. Trump called for the NBC television network's broadcasting license to be withdrawn after NBC stations reported stories he did not like. "With all of the Fake News coming out of NBC and the Networks, at what point is it appropriate to challenge their License? Bad for country," he tweeted in October 2017. In September 2018, he wrote, "Look at their license?" referring again to NBC.

The Federal Communications Commission, which is an independent federal agency that is not governed by a presidential administration, issues broadcast licenses. However, the agency issues licenses not to large television networks, but to hundreds of individual television stations. Therefore, it has no power to take away NBC's or any other network's license. But when a president issues such threats, it encourages people to be suspicious about television networks he personally does not like.

WORLDWIDE DANGER TO JOURNALISTS

We live in a country where the press has had the right to free expression for more than two hundred years. We may forget this is a privilege of a democratic government, one we don't want to lose. In the United States, journalists are rarely jailed and they don't have to worry daily about being murdered. In several other countries in the world, they do.

The Committee to Protect Journalists (CPJ) monitors how many journalists have been jailed each year and how many have been murdered because of the views they express. In 2018, more than 250 journalists went to jail because of the stories they pursued. Many of them were charged with aiding terrorist or other organizations that opposed their governments. Twenty-eight were charged specifically with spreading false news. Nineteen of these were in Egypt. Turkey had taken the most reporters prisoner: sixty-eight. China had imprisoned forty-seven; Saudi Arabia had sixteen reporters jailed on December 2018, including four women who had written about women's rights. The CPJ survey does not include journalists who are arrested and released within the year.

Even more alarming, fifty-six journalists were killed in 2018, including nine press people in Kabul, Afghanistan, on April 30. The journalists had been running to report on a suicide bombing of government buildings by the terrorist group ISIS. A second suicide bomber joined them, pretending to be a member of the media. When his bomb went off, the journalists were killed. One of them was a photographer for a French news agency. "This tragedy reminds us of the danger that our teams continually face . . . and the essential role journalists play for democracy. Journalists were targeted by this attack," said the chairman of the news agency.

Journalists face violence from terrorists and drug cartels, but they can also be targets of governments they criticize. Jamal Khashoggi, a Saudi Arabian journalist critical of his country, who was a columnist for the *Washington Post*, was murdered on October 2, 2018. He had been living in the United States but had visited the Saudi consulate in Istanbul, Turkey. He was killed there, it is believed, by representatives of the Saudi government. Suggestions from any government leader that violence toward reporters is appropriate only increases the danger from doing their jobs.

In July 2018, the White House did not allow Kaitlan Collins, a correspondent for CNN, to attend a press conference open to all journalists in the Rose Garden. On November 7, the White House revoked the press badge for another CNN reporter, banning him from all White House press conferences. The reporter, Jim Acosta, had refused to stop asking questions about topics the president did not want to address. Taking back Acosta's credentials went against the principle of press freedom. On November 16, a federal judge—one appointed by President Trump—ordered that Acosta's press badge be returned so that he could again attend White House briefings.

After the White House revoked CNN reporter Jim Acosta's press badge on November 7, 2018 (so he couldn't attend news conferences there), a federal judge ordered that it be restored. Here Acosta appears at an informal press conference in front of the White House on November 16, 2018.

Trump has advocated bringing back the "fairness doctrine," established in 1949. There have been congressional attempts, often by Democrats, to reinstate the doctrine. Significant opposition has come from conservative, right-wing stations that do not want to devote time to opinions different from their own. These stations often support Trump's policies. Requiring the fairness doctrine again would likely mean more negative airtime about him, not less.

In August 2018, the *Boston Globe* put out a call to all newspapers, "liberal and conservative, large and small—to join us" to address President Trump's frequent attacks on the news media. The paper received responses from more than 350 news organizations, agreeing with the *Globe* that Trump's "'relentless assault on the free press has dangerous consequences.'"

"Lies are antithetical to an informed citizenry, responsible for self-governance," said a *Globe* editorial. "The greatness of America is dependent on the role of a free press to speak the truth to the powerful. To label the press 'the enemy of the people' is as un-American as it is dangerous to the civic compact we have shared for more than two centuries," since the Bill of Rights was passed.

The *Hartford Courant* in Connecticut wrote, "We're at high school football games, at zoning hearings, and the latest show so that we can help you decide if it's worth going. And when the unthinkable happens and 6-year-olds are gunned down at school, we wrestle with our own shock and grief while telling a stunned state the story. Doesn't sound like the nefarious work of enemies

LEGAL OR NOT?

In 1949, the Federal Communications Commission (FCC) proclaimed the "fairness doctrine." Since there was a limit to the number of radio broadcast outlets the commission could authorize, it wanted to make sure that listeners would hear all points of view. The fairness doctrine also applied to television stations that transmitted over the air. They had to "devote reasonable attention to the coverage of controversial issues of pubic importance." They also had to provide a "reasonable, although not necessarily equal" chance to opposing sides to let listeners know their points of view. So if a liberal commentator, for example, explained the reasons why immigration might help the United States, an anti-immigration speaker had to be given airtime as well.

In 1964, Reverend Billy James Hargis denounced journalist Fred Cook, who had written a book attacking Barry Goldwater, the Republican candidate for president. Hargis was a Christian evangelist preacher and dedicated anti-communist. He claimed that Cook worked for a communist publication. Hargis's program was broadcast by the Red Lion Broadcasting Company, a conservative radio station in Pennsylvania. Cook asked for equal time under the fairness doctrine to refute what Hargis had said. The radio station said no. It claimed forcing the station to broadcast what it did not want to was a violation of the First Amendment. In 1969, the case went to the Supreme Court as *Red Lion Broadcasting Co. v. Federal Communications Commission*. The Court voted in favor of Cook, upholding the fairness doctrine as legal and not in violation of First Amendment Rights.

But in 1987, Congress repealed the fairness doctrine. The government felt that radio stations, like other businesses, should not be closely regulated. It wanted to encourage competition and competing views by freeing radio stations from the need to present both sides, even if they only agreed with one of them.

After radio was deregulated, the number of conservative radio talk shows grew. Rush Limbaugh was the best known of the "shock jocks," who wanted to offend their listeners. He has called himself "the most dangerous man in America." Now conservative talk shows fill YouTube. There are liberal talk shows, but they have never been as popular as the conservative ones.

of the American people. Sounds like people who care about the community where they own homes, pay taxes, send their kids to school. Who believe, simply, that the truth can help us all lead better lives."

"During the tumultuous summer of 1963," wrote the *Columbian-Progress* in Mississippi, "the KKK burned crosses" at the home of Oliver Emmerich, a conservative Mississippi newspaper founder. "The paper's response was a simple yet courageous and effective one: Publish stories about that domestic terrorism on its front page, the very thing the attackers meant to prevent from happening."

Silencing the press is "the attack potential dictators always make," wrote the *Plymouth Review* in Wisconsin. "Shut down or strangle newspapers like ours, silence radio stations, blur or subvert TV stations, and—in these digital times—boost unverifiable 'social media' . . . where people may only see what they want to see, hear what they want to hear, say what they want to say."

In 2019, President Trump continued his attacks on the press he disliked. In a speech in July, he declared, "We certainly don't want to stifle free speech, but . . . I don't think that the mainstream media is free speech either because it's so crooked. It's so dishonest . . . Free speech is not when you see something good and then you purposely write bad. To me, that's very dangerous speech . . . But that's not free speech."

"The Failing @nytimes, & ratings challenged @CNN, will do anything possible to see our Country fail! They are truly The Enemy of the People!" the president tweeted on June 9, 2019.

This New York Daily News *front page of February 25, 2017, conveys the newspaper's opinion that President Trump was violating the right of freedom of the press through his words and actions. The headline was an immediate response to the White House barring the attendance of several journalists from a press briefing the day before.*

Being told to believe only in the press one leader agrees with and to ignore criticism is not part of the democracy the Founding Fathers envisioned. President Trump once stated, in October 2017, that "it's frankly disgusting the way the press is able to write whatever they want to write." But protecting any American's printed news or opinion—"to write whatever they want to write"—was exactly what the First Amendment was meant to guarantee.

Not everyone in the Trump administration has belittled the press. Before he became Trump's vice president, Mike Pence cosponsored a law that would protect a reporter's right to not name sources. As vice president, he said on October 30, 2018, "I do believe that the only check on government power in real time is a free and independent press . . . It was at the core of the American founding, and it's a core American principle."

But these are not the words that the world hears and remembers. The loudest voice is the president's, and as Christopher Wallace said to Trump on Fox News, "You're seen around the world as a beacon for repression." A government official in Myanmar claimed there were no minority groups being persecuted in his country. He called it "fake news." It has become a fashionable way for dictators to dismiss the criticisms of the press. Once, the United States was known as the leader of the free world. It was ready to go to war, as President Woodrow Wilson said, to keep the world "safe for democracy." Now, in attacking our own press, we need to ask, again, just what a free press in a democracy means.

CHAPTER 9

KEEPING THE PRESS SAFE FOR DEMOCRACY

We are at a time in our history when Americans on all sides of politics—Democrats, Republicans, liberals, conservatives—tend to only read or listen to news media that support their views. We are much more likely to argue with than to listen to each other. If we believe strongly about something, it is hard to change our minds by presenting facts. The internet is the major source of information now. Yet the internet conveys much more opinion than it does factual news. Everyone becomes empowered to comment on government policies without necessarily giving sources, evidence, or credentials. Americans can look to the media that help them feel comfortable about holding their own opinions.

The continued use of the phrase "fake news" confirms Trump supporters who doubt or dismiss what is reported by newspapers, broadcast media, and internet sites that question the statements and policies of the president. But liberals and Democrats distrust conservative media as much as conservatives distrust liberal

Democrats who attended the Kansas State Democratic Convention on February 25, 2017, hold signs expressing their opinions about the value of a free press.

media. They can find support for their views in the media that can be counted on to dislike the Trump administration's policies. These include MSNBC television, CNN, and the *New York Times*, sources the president attacks. They reinforce the beliefs of those who hold negative opinions about the president.

One of the newspapers Trump criticizes is the *Washington Post*, which wrote in April 2019 that he was on record as having lied ten thousand times since he became president in 2017. Another *Post* article charged: "He made a series of false claims about immigration, such as 'open borders bring tremendous crime' (there is no documented link between illegal immigration and crime). He claimed he passed the biggest tax cut in history (no) and he said he had cut the estate tax to 'zero' (no)."

But if one follows different news sources, she or he will find that conservative media have also criticized Trump for lying. "Fox Business host Neil Cavuto said . . . that President Trump was 'lying' when he claimed that U.S. tariffs on Chinese goods had taken in $100 billion in revenue for the [U.S.] government," reported the *Washington Examiner* on May 14, 2019.

Cohosts Steve Doocy (center) and Ainsley Earhardt (right) chat with Sarah Huckabee Sanders (left) on Fox & Friends, *a news and talk program that gives positive coverage to President Trump and his policies. Sanders, former press secretary to Trump, joined Fox News as a political commentator after leaving the White House.*

Fox & Friends, a morning news and commentary program, is known to be a favorite of President Trump's, and it routinely supports his statements even when they are misleading or untrue. But in the spring of 2019, Trump began criticizing other Fox News programs that were not supportive of him. "Watching @FoxNews weekend anchors is worse than watching low ratings Fake News @CNN . . . and the crew of degenerate Comcast (NBC/MSNBC)," he tweeted in July. "But @FoxNews, who failed in getting the very BORING Dem[ocratic] debates, is now loading up with Democrats & even using Fake unsourced @nytimes as a 'source' of information . . . @FoxNews is changing fast, but they forgot the people who got them there!"

It is easy to quickly change opinions, then change them back again, on social media. News moves so swiftly, and so much information is available on the internet, that it can be overwhelming. One might think that because there is plenty of information at hand, journalists can research in-depth articles on the topics they feel are important. They can gather facts and evidence as the muckraking writers did at the end of the nineteenth century. But it takes a lot of time, money, and dedication to research thoroughly or to expose corruption that could embarrass government and business.

Most media outlets, knowing the public is most interested in fast and breaking news, do not put their resources into long-term investigation. Print newspapers, especially, do not have the money for specialized research. Traditionally, their main source of income has been paid-for advertising. But businesses are now spending more of their advertising budget on placing ads on the internet. The more readers click on and share a website, the more the publisher of that website can charge for its ads. Advertisers look for websites that they think their buyers will be attracted to. Newspaper websites carry ads, but even the money from that advertising revenue is not enough to support a large amount of investigative journalism.

That leaves readers and viewers to judge on their own whether what they see and hear seems true, not what they are told by other

CAN YOU TELL IF YOUR NEWS IS ACCURATE?

Since conflicting news, information, and opinions come from many places, how can readers judge what is true?

 See if the news piece names a source. Be careful when you read or hear something that says "people say," or "many people think," without telling you who those people are.

 Check to see if other news outlets agree with what you are reading; or if they don't agree, why, and where the difference is.

 Ask if what you are reading or listening to presents diverse points of view. If it continually leaves out African Americans, women, immigrants, farmers and ranchers, the Christian right, the unemployed, or any other group, you can actively look for other sources that express these points of view before you make up your mind about what is accurate.

 Search what are considered reliable sites—those posted by U.S. government agencies, for example, or universities, or respected, nonpartisan organizations like the Pew Research Center, which compiles statistics on global problems. There are documents, statistics, budgets, and other verifiable material that anyone can access in a book or online.

 Notice whether an article or news broadcast places the information reported in a political and historical context. One value of the press has always been to help Americans interpret the overwhelming barrage of information that hits them every day. Do the interpretations seem reasonable and fair, and are they backed up by facts?

Students from Annandale High School in Virginia attend a class on fighting fake news in Washington, D.C., in August 2017.

people or the press. One doesn't have to take an internet post, a television broadcast, or a newspaper article on faith. Statements can be checked. Tweets, press briefings, and speeches are on record. They are filmed and recorded. The White House itself posts the transcripts of speeches.

One can check facts and other sources, however, and still not agree with a news article, an editorial, or a radio or television broadcast. But if one believes in freedom of the press, she or he accepts that other people have the same right as they do to say what they believe, even if it seems unpleasant, dishonest, or dangerous. Remember what Supreme Court Justice Oliver Wendell Holmes Jr.

wrote in *United States v. Schwimmer* (1929): "If there is any principle of the Constitution that more imperatively calls for attachment [belief in] than any other, it is the principle of free thought—not free thought for those who agree with us but freedom for the thought that we hate." Fox News and CNN, conservative radio programs and the *New York Times*—even presidents—have the same right that all Americans have to express their opinions. Every American has the right to disagree.

There is a difference, though, between having rights and having those rights honored or preserved. Many Americans think we have the freest press in the world. Reporters Without Borders, an organization promoting press freedom, ranks 180 countries in terms of how free their news media are every year. In the 2019 ratings, the United States came in at number 48. Norway ranked number one, with the other Scandinavian countries in the top ten. North Korea ranked as 179, with Syria, China, Vietnam, and Sudan in the bottom ten. The rankings are based on several factors, including how great a range of opinions is expressed in the media; how independent the media is from government, business, and other institutional sources; legal restrictions against journalists; and how much reporters face abuse and violence.

The 2019 report explained the drop in ranking (it was 45 in 2018) of the United States. "President Trump continued to spout his notorious anti-press rhetoric, disparaging and attacking the media at a national level," read the report. In addition, "Journalists reporting on Trump rallies continued to be harangued and

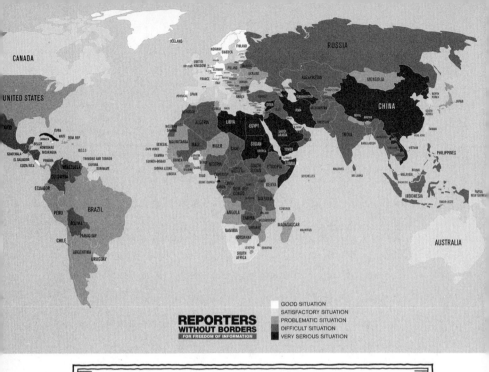

REPORTERS
WITHOUT BORDERS
FOR FREEDOM OF INFORMATION

GOOD SITUATION
SATISFACTORY SITUATION
PROBLEMATIC SITUATION
DIFFICULT SITUATION
VERY SERIOUS SITUATION

This map, published by Reporters Without Borders, shows the status of press freedom in countries worldwide in 2019. The United States is considered to have a "problematic situation"—that is, while the press has many freedoms, it also encounters barriers to confidential government information and has recently been disparaged and discredited by the president.

even physically accosted by attendees. Local and national newsrooms received bomb threats . . . Journalists covering the Trump administration were denied access to information and events of public interest . . . Attempted access denials extended to local politics too, as journalists across the country were refused entry to midterm election events and even polling stations."

America's Founding Fathers envisioned a press that would be freer than Britain's, the country they won independence from. They also envisioned one where reasoned debate would lead people to correct solutions. This has not always been the case. But as imperfect and contradictory as the press has been for more than two hundred years—critical, feisty, persistent, inaccurate, even hateful, valuing making money above revealing the truth—imagine our country without it. Imagine a world where the only information that came to you was approved by a government, whether honest or corrupt. Imagine a world where minorities had no voice. Imagine a world where Americans had no power to change harmful government policies and agendas. Imagine a world where you doubted everything—everything you read, everything you saw—without trusting your own common sense.

Americans are lucky to have the liberties that they do. We may go through periods when the press is under attack, yet we have never censored it completely. But freedom of the press will only remain a mainstay of our law and our society as long as we believe in the principle, practice it, and value it.

TIMELINE OF KEY EVENTS

1439: Johannes Gutenberg is the first person in the Western world to use movable type, starting a revolution in printing. His method will be used throughout the eighteenth century.

1704: The *Boston News-Letter* is the first newspaper in the American colonies to successfully publish for several years. In 1719, others will begin printing.

1735: Printer John Peter Zenger is accused of printing libelous material about the colonial governor of New York. He is found not guilty by a jury.

1765: The English Parliament passes the Stamp Act, calling for a tax on paper in the colonies. After colonial opposition, the act is repealed in 1766.

1775: The American Revolution begins with the Battles of Lexington and Concord. It ends in 1783.

1776: Leading American colonists issue the Declaration of Independence.

1788: The Constitution of the United States is approved.

1791: The Bill of Rights, with the First Amendment including freedom of the press, is added to the Constitution.

1798: Congress, at the urging of President John Adams, passes the Sedition Act, which makes the author of any negative comments about the majority party in power subject to fines and imprisonment.

1800: Thomas Jefferson is elected president over John Adams after a vicious partisan battle in the press.

1828: Andrew Jackson is elected president over John Quincy Adams after partisan attacks on both men in the press.

1835: The New York *Sun* reports in six articles that men are living on the moon. It is a hoax—"fake news"—designed to excite readers and sell more newspapers. The *Sun*'s circulation greatly increases.

1843: Thomas Howe creates a steam-powered rotary press that makes printing newspapers much faster.

1861: The Civil War between the northern Union and the southern Confederacy begins. After four months, the first newspapers opposing President Abraham Lincoln's policies are denied the right to be sent through the mail.

1862: President Lincoln issues the preliminary Emancipation Proclamation, freeing the slaves held in the Confederacy. The proclamation becomes official on January 1, 1863. It is very controversial.

1863: Union general Ambrose Burnside stops publication of the anti-Lincoln *Chicago Times.* Lincoln orders that the paper be allowed to publish again.

1885: The first automatic typesetting machine—the linotype—is invented.

1890s: The yellow press newspapers, the *New York World* and the *New York Journal,* use sensational stories to compete for readers.

The "muckrakers," a group of progressive writers and reporters, expose corruption in government and business, leading to laws that protect the American people.

The presses roll at the New York Times in 1942. Newspapers were printed this way from the early twentieth century until the rise of digital, computer-based printing.

1896: Adolph Ochs takes over the *New York Times*, promising readers a reliable, factual newspaper that does not deal in sensational reporting.

1898: The U.S.S. *Maine* explodes in Havana Harbor. Encouraged by the yellow journalism press, the United States begins the Spanish-American War. Americans are victorious after five months.

1916: A very small group of listeners hears the first radio broadcast in the United States, of the 1916 election results. Radio had been invented and improved in the late nineteenth century and early years of the twentieth century.

1917: The United States enters World War I, which had been raging in Europe since 1914.

Congress passes the Espionage Act, which bans anything printed that advocates against the war or the United States government. The act is still in effect today.

1918: Congress passes the Sedition Act, calling for the arrest of anyone who uses negative language about the "form of government of the United States, or the Constitution." It is repealed in 1921.

1919: Socialist Victor Berger is convicted under the Espionage Act for criticizing America's participation in World War I. The Supreme Court overturns his conviction in 1921.

The Supreme Court hears *Schenck v. United States* and confirms Charles Schenck's conviction for speaking out against the draft.

The Supreme Court hears *Abrams v. United States*, upholding the conviction of Jacob Abrams and four other defendants for distributing leaflets calling for strikes in American munitions plants.

1923: The Supreme Court hears *Gitlow v. New York*, upholding Benjamin Gitlow's conviction for distribution of communist materials. This case is the first time the Supreme Court rules on a state court decision concerning freedom of the press based on the "equal protection of the laws" clause of the Fourteenth Amendment (1868).

1927: The first electronic television is invented.

1931: The Supreme Court rules in *Near v. Minnesota* that "prior restraint" is illegal. The government cannot stop publication of a news article before it is printed.

1933: President Franklin Roosevelt begins giving Sunday "Fireside Chats" on the radio to explain government policies and actions to Americans. These continue through World War II and are very popular.

1941: The United States enters World War II after the Japanese bombing of Pearl Harbor. Within days, the Office of Censorship is established. It encourages media to voluntarily censor any information that might hurt the war effort.

1942: William Dudley Pelley is arrested and convicted of sedition for publishing fascist writings.

1943: The U.S. government allows *Life* magazine to publish the first photograph of dead American soldiers. Before that, photographs showing the brutal realities of war had been censored.

1949: The Federal Communications Commission (FCC) proclaims the "fairness doctrine," which calls for radio and television stations to give people who are criticized politically airtime to present their point of view. The Supreme Court upholds the doctrine in 1969, in *Red Lion Broadcasting Co. v. Federal Communications Commission.* Congress repeals the doctrine in 1987.

1950: The Korean War (1950–1953) begins, with the United States providing 90 percent of the military forces. The American media will start criticizing the American strategy after a series of losses to North Korean troops.

1960s: In the early 1960s, scientists and government begin research on what will become the internet.

1963: Television news shows the brutal treatment by police of civil rights demonstrators in Birmingham, Alabama. Violent scenes increase support in the North for laws guaranteeing civil rights to African Americans.

1964: The Supreme Court hears *New York Times Co. v. Sullivan*, involving the charge that an ad placed in the *Times* by civil rights leaders had libeled Alabama officials. The Court finds in favor of the *Times*, believing the newspaper had exercised its right to press freedom.

1965: The first U.S. combat troops arrive in Vietnam, and American bombing of North Vietnam begins. The United States had first sent advisory troops to the area in 1955 to support the South Vietnamese in a civil war with the North.

1968: North Vietnamese troops, aided by China, begin the Tet Offensive. They are able to reach Saigon (now Ho Chi Minh City), the South Vietnamese capital. Although the North Vietnamese are forced to retreat, Americans see this as a loss, not a victory, increasing support for an immediate end to the war.

1968: Richard Nixon defeats Hubert Humphrey for the presidency. Although Nixon vows to gradually withdraw American troops from Vietnam, he escalates the war in 1970 by invading Cambodia.

The Supreme Court hears *Tinker v. Des Moines Independent Community School District,* a case in which students were suspended from school for wearing black armbands to protest the Vietnam War. The Court rules in favor of the students, upholding the right of free speech.

1971: The *New York Times* and the *Washington Post* print parts of the Pentagon Papers, a confidential study of the United States' involvement in Vietnam. The government wants to prevent publication. In *New York Times Co. v. United States,* the newspapers win a victory as the court rules it is their First Amendment right to print the study.

The first technology for email is developed.

1988: The Supreme Court rules in *Hazelwood School District v. Kuhlmeier* that public school officials have the right to censor articles in a student newspaper that may not be appropriate for younger children.

1990: Tim Berners-Lee writes the program necessary to use the World Wide Web.

1991: The United States leads an air attack against Iraq in the Persian Gulf War (1990–1991). During this war, journalists are organized into "pools" assigned to military officers who escort them to chosen sites as they report on the war.

1994: The first blog is said to have been posted.

2001: Two towers of the World Trade Center in New York and part of the Pentagon are destroyed, and a plane crashes in Pennsylvania, in terrorist attacks organized by al-Qaeda on September 11. The event will become known as "9/11."

The United States begins bombing Afghanistan, where al-Qaeda's leaders are being supported by the Taliban, a militant Islamic group.

2003: The Iraq War (2003–2011) begins. The United States claims that it is preventing Iraq from continuing to develop weapons of mass destruction (WMDs), though none are ever found.

2003: Journalists covering the Iraq War are "embedded"—placed in military units and allowed to go with them to combat zones to report.

2004: Facebook goes online.

2005: YouTube goes online.

Judith Miller, then a *New York Times* reporter, is jailed for eighty-five days for refusing to reveal her source to a grand jury.

2006: Twitter debuts.

2010: WikiLeaks, a whistle-blowing media organization, publishes classified documents online about the wars in Afghanistan and Iraq. In 2019, Julian Assange, WikiLeaks' founder, is charged under the 1917 Espionage Act.

2016: During the presidential election campaign between Hillary Clinton and Donald Trump, fake websites about them are common on the internet. Donald Trump wins the presidency.

2017: Trump frequently uses Twitter to attack what he calls the "fake news" media—those articles, broadcasts, and postings that he does not like.

President Trump labels the media he does not agree with "enemies of the people."

2018: More than 250 journalists worldwide are jailed and fifty-six are murdered, according to the Committee to Protect Journalists. One of those killed is Jamal Khashoggi, a columnist for the *Washington Post*, who had criticized his country, Saudi Arabia.

The White House revokes CNN reporter Jim Acosta's press badge, so he cannot attend press conferences. A federal judge orders that the badge be reinstated.

2019: Reporters Without Borders ranks the United States as number 48 out of 180 countries for its policies and actions to promote freedom of the press.

NOTES

Full bibliographic information for books cited in the Notes can be found in the Selected Bibliography.

INTRODUCTION

3 "The principle of free thought . . . that we hate": Lewis, *Freedom for the Thought That We Hate*, 37.

4 "Freedom of speech . . . society is dissolved": "Great American Thinkers on Free Speech," *Saturday Evening Post*, January 16, 2015, www.saturdayevening post.com/2015/01/great-american-thinkers-free-speech.

4 "There is nothing . . . *of the People's Liberties*": Levy, *Emergence of a Free Press*, 67.

5 "suffer men . . . oppressed people": Abernathy, *American Government*, 77.

7 "vigorous Executive . . . an elective one": "Madison Debates: June 1," The Avalon Project, Lillian Goldman Law Library, Yale Law School, avalon.law.yale .edu/18th_century/debates_601.asp.

8 "political iniquity . . . upon the United States": Chris Weigant, "George Washington's Biggest Critic," *Huffington Post*, February 20, 2012, updated December 6, 2017, www.huffpost.com/entry/george-washington-critics_b_ 1289485.

8–9 "Every president . . . himself as well": Ronald Reagon, "Remarks at the Annual White House Correspondents Association Dinner, April 21, 1988," Ronald Reagan Presidential Library & Museum, www.reaganlibrary.gov /research/speeches/042188d.

12 "alternative facts": Eric Bradner, "Conway: Trump White House Offered 'Alternative Facts' on Crowd Size," CNN.com, January 23, 2017, www.cnn .com/2017/01/22/politics/kellyanne-conway-alternative-facts/index.html.

CHAPTER 1: THE EIGHTEENTH CENTURY: PARTISAN PRESS AND REVOLUTION

17 "If people shall . . . looked upon as a crime": Levy, *Emergence of a Free Press*, 9.

18 "a seditious person . . . wickedly and maliciously": Professor Douglas O. Linder, "The Trial of John Peter Zenger: An Account," *Famous Trials*, UMKC School of Law, www.famous-trials.com/zenger/87-home.

19 "truth . . . than falsehood": Levy, *Emergence of a Free Press*, 42.

19 "It is natural . . . cause of liberty": Linder, "The Trial of John Peter Zenger," www.famous-trials.com/zenger/87-home.

22 Newspapers in the colonies: "Colonial Print Culture," *The News Media and the Making of America, 1730–1865*, American Antiquarian Society, americanantiquarian.org/earlyamericannewsmedia/exhibits/show /news-in-colonial-america/colonial-print-culture.

22 "News do[es] not appear . . . political essays": "The History of Printing in America: With a Biography of Printers, and an Account of Newspapers: To Which Is Prefixed a Concise View of the Discovery and Progress of the Art in Other Parts of the World: in Two Volumes," Archive.org, archive.org/stream /historyofprintin02inthom/historyofprintin02inthom_djvu.txt.

23 "filled with every falsehood . . . to sedition": "Until the Stamp Act Was Repealed the Colonists Must . . . ," University of Florida, Course Hero, www.coursehero.com/file/pb0om2/Until-the-Stamp-Act-was-repealed-the -colonists-must-resist-it-with-all-the.

24 "a STAMP in . . . [organs]": "The Tombstone Edition: *Pennsylvania Journal*, October 31, 1765, *Journal of the American Revolution*, June 15, 2015, allthingslib- erty.com/2015/06/the-tombstone-edition-pennsylvania-journal -october-31-1765/.

24 "*I must Die* . . . lose my Freedom": Arthur M. Schlesinger, "The Colonial Newspapers and the Stamp Act," *New England Quarterly* 8, no. 1 (March 1935), JSTOR, www.jstor.org/stable/359430.

25 "fired Bullets . . . save his life": "Rough Music: Popular Political Expression

in Colonial America," userpages.umbc.edu/~bouton/History407
/RoughMusicDocument.htm.

25 "one of his fine Horses poisoned": "Rough Music."

25 "was confined & bound . . . threatened to be sent to": "Rough Music."

26–27 "We are determined . . . support the King": "Anti-Loyalist Broadsides &
Blank Allegiance Forms, 1775–1776: A Selection," America in Class, Making the
Revolution: America, 1763–1791, National Humanities Center, americainclass
.org/sources/makingrevolution/rebellion/text2/loyalistsbroadsides.pdf.

27 "The [thirteen] colonies . . . a very difficult enterprise": "From John Adams
to Hezekiah Niles, 13 February 1818," *Founders Online*, National Archives,
founders.archives.gov/documents/Adams/99-02-02-6854.

27 "Freedom of the Press . . . despotic [tyrannical] Governments": Powe Jr., *The
Fourth Estate and the Constitution*, 26.

28 "The liberty of the press . . . to be restrained": Powe Jr., 26.

CHAPTER 2: CONGRESS DOES MAKE A LAW . . .

31 "There is nothing that the people . . . they dislike its conduct": Powe Jr.,
The Fourth Estate and the Constitution, 35.

33 "this bill must be considered . . . from those of the administration":
Powe Jr., 60.

33 "any false, scandalous . . . people of the United States": "Transcript of Alien
and Sedition Acts (1798)," OurDocuments.gov, www.ourdocuments.gov
/doc.php?flash=false&doc=16&page=transcript#no-3.

33 "continual grasp of power . . . selfish avarice": Lewis, *Freedom for the Thought
That We Hate*, 13.

34–35 "The constitutional power . . . every other right": *The Virginia Report of
1799–1800, Touching the Alien and Sedition Laws*, Richmond, VA : J. W. Randolph,
1850, 233, Hathi Trust Digital Library, babel.hathitrust.org/cgi
/pt?id=nyp.33433090214291&view=1up&seq=228.

35 "strange compound of ignorance . . . sensibility of a woman":
"Hideous Hermaphroditical Character (Spurious Quotation)," Thomas Jefferson
Foundation, Monticello.org, www.monticello.org/site/research-and-collections
/hideous-hermaphroditical-character-spurious-quotation.

35 "weakling" . . . "atheist" . . . "coward": Kerwin Swint, "Adams vs. Jefferson: The Birth of Negative Campaigning in the U.S.," *Mental Floss*, September 9, 2012, mentalfloss.com/article/12487/adams-vs-jefferson-birth-negative-campaigning-us.

35–37 "The basis of our governments . . . prefer the latter": "Extract from Thomas Jefferson to Edward Carrington," January 16, 1787, Thomas Jefferson Foundation, Monticello.org, tjrs.monticello.org/letter/1289.

37 "Nothing can now be believed . . . lies of the day": "Image 2 of Thomas Jefferson to John Norvell, June 11, 1807," The Thomas Jefferson Papers at the Library of Congress, loc.gov, www.loc.gov/resource/mtj1.038_0592_0594/?sp=2&st=text.

37 "If there should be any disloyalty . . . stern repression": Osborne, *Come on in, America*, 84.

38 "Every letter . . . nonmailable": Osborne, 84.

38 "Why, Senators . . . and the World": Cooke, *Reporting the War*, 91–93.

40 "any disloyal, profane . . . the Constitution": "The Sedition Act of 1918," www.digitalhistory.uh.edu/disp_textbook.cfm?smtID=3&psid=3903.

40 "The chief criticism . . . in the future": "Censorship Plan in New Spy Bill Stirs Opponents," *Bridgeport Evening Farmer*, April 13, 1917, Connecticut Digital Newspaper Project, ctdigitalnewspaperproject.org/2016/07/free-speech-seditious-speech-in-world-war-i-era-connecticut.

41 "All seditionists . . . American citizen": Cooke, *Reporting the War*, 101.

42 877 people were convicted: Shirley J. Burton, "The Espionage and Sedition Acts of 1917 and 1918: Sectional Interpretations in the United States District Courts of Illinois," *Illinois Historical Journal* 87, no. 1 (Spring 1994): 45, JSTOR.org, www.jstor.org/stable/40192770.

42 "Long Live . . . on the Constitution": "Landmark Supreme Court Cases," National Constitution Center, Google Arts & Culture, artsandculture.google.com/exhibit/aQISuVpqYWBkKA.

43 "We admit that . . . right to prevent": "*Schenck v. United States* (1919)," The WWW Virtual Library, www.vlib.us/amdocs/texts/schenk.htm.

45 "Even if their . . . in this country": *Abrams v. United States*, Legal Information Institute, Cornell Law School, www.law.cornell.edu/supremecourt/text/250/616.

45 "The principle of . . . save the country": *Abrams v. United States.*

47 "It is a fundamental . . . organized government": *Gitlow v. People*, Legal Information Institute, Cornell Law School, www.law.cornell.edu/supremecourt /text/268/652.

47 "It is said that this manifesto . . . enthusiasm for the result": *Gitlow v. People.*

49 "no state shall . . . protection of the laws": "14th Amendment," Legal Information Institute, Cornell Law School, www.law.cornell.edu/constitution /amendmentxiv.

CHAPTER 3: NEWS, POLITICS, AND WAR IN THE NINETEENTH CENTURY

51–53 "There is no charge . . . annals of our republic": Mark Cheathem, "Frontiersman or Southern Gentleman? Newspaper Coverage of Andrew Jackson During the 1828 Presidential Campaign," *Readex Report* 9, no. 3, September 2014, www.readex.com/readex-report/frontiersman-or-southern -gentleman-newspaper-coverage-andrew-jackson-during-1828.

53 "The man, who . . . Candidate for President": "Personal Attacks Levied Against Andrew Jackson," *Sign of the Times*, August 23, 1828, Timothy Hughes Rare & Early Newspapers, www.rarenewspapers.com/view/571892?imagelist=1.

54 "As long as our government . . . worth defending": "First Inaugural Address of Andrew Jackson: Wednesday, March 4, 1829," The Avalon Project, Lillian Goldman Library, Yale Law School, avalon.law.yale.edu/19th_century /jackson1.asp.

54–55 "It has abused no privilege . . . National Administration": Cooke, *Reporting the War*, 49.

56 350 correspondents . . . 150 from the South: Reynolds and Van Tuyll, *The Greenwood Library of American War Reporting: Civil War*, 7.

58 "Certain journals . . . by the Constitution": Cooke, 51.

58 "the city . . . Anti-Slavery sentiments": Reynolds and Van Tuyll, *The Greenwood Library of American War Reporting: Civil War*, 169.

58–59 "bloody" . . . "barbarous" . . . "racial fanaticism": "Civil War Tested Lincoln's Tolerance for Free Speech, Press," Freedom Forum Institute, February 11, 2009, www.freedomforuminstitute.org/2009/02/11/civil-war-tested -lincolns-tolerance-for-free-speech-press.

59 "We have only anticipation . . . profound regret": Reynolds and Van Tuyll, *The Greenwood Library of American War Reporting: Civil War*, 174.

59–60 "If the Proclamation . . . industry and thrift": "The President's Proclamation," *New York Times*, January 3, 1863, *New York Times* Archives, www.nytimes.com/1863/01/03/archives/the-presidents-proclamation.html.

60 "Newspapers were full . . . hereby suppressed": "Civil War Tested Lincoln's Tolerance for Free Speech, Press."

60 "Freedom of discussion . . . in time of peace": "Civil War Tested Lincoln's Tolerance."

61 "Whereas there has been wickedly . . . further publication therefrom": Abraham Lincoln, letter to John A. Dix, *Collected Works of Abraham Lincoln, Volume 7*, 348, The Abraham Lincoln Association, quod.lib.umich.edu/l/lincoln /lincoln7/1:773?rgn=div1;view=fulltext.

65 "Destruction of the War Ship . . . an Enemy": "Destruction of the War Ship Maine Was the Work of an Enemy," *New York Journal and Advertiser*, February 17, 1894, posted by bbebn, November 24, 2010, Comm455/History of Journalism, historyofjournalism.onmason.com/2010/11/24/destruction-of-the-war -ship-maine-was-the-work-of-an-enemy.

65 "*Maine* Explosion" . . . "by an Enemy": "Maine Explosion Caused by Bomb or Torpedo?" *New York World*, February 17, 1894, New York Public Library Digital Collections, digitalcollections.nypl.org/items/84ea964f-4861 -b09d-e040-e00a18066a1d.

66 "The firing-drill . . . volleys of ammunition": Tyler Wilson, "U.S. and Spanish Newspapers and the Coverage of the Land Campaign of Cuba in the Spanish-American War: June 7 to July 16, 1898," Honors Thesis, Paper 2521, Western Michigan University October 17, 2014, p. 13, pdfs.semanticscholar. org/8e5c/ce70cbcf7ce5edfd4bcec5919ded094c3c30.pdf.

67 "clean, dignified" . . . "pure-minded people": "Adolph S. Ochs Dead at 77; Publisher of Times Since 1896," *New York Times* Obituary, April 9, 1935, On This Day, *New York Times* Archive, archive.nytimes.com/www.nytimes.com /learning/general/onthisday/bday/0312.html.

70 "Now it is very necessary . . . filth on the floor": "American Rhetoric, Top 100 Speeches," www.americanrhetoric.com/speeches/teddyroosevelt muckrake.htm.

CHAPTER 4: TWENTIETH-CENTURY PRESIDENTS, WAR, AND THE NEWS MEDIA

74 "Will anyone hearing . . . being received": "Westinghouse Broadcasting Company News Release on the 'History of Broadcasting and KDKA Radio,' circa 1960," ExplorePAHistory.com, explorepahistory.com/odocument.php ?docId=1-4-288.

77 "To a free people" . . . "his own censor": Byron Price, "Governmental Censorship in War-Time," *The American Political Science Review* 36, no. 5 (October 1942): 837, JSTOR.org, www.jstor.org/stable/1949286.

78 "It is a heartening example . . . are not seditious": Byron Price, 848.

78 "To rationalize . . . solicited war with": "*United States v. Pelley*, 132 F.2d 170 (7th Cir. 1942)," Court Listener, www.courtlistener.com/opinion/1480872 /united-states-v-pelley.

79 "When we get through . . . Germany was nothing": "Coughlin Quotes on Politics: Anti-Semitism," FatherCoughlin.org, www.fathercoughlin.org /father-coughlin-quotes.html.

80 "to embarrass and defeat . . . prosecute the war": Stone, *Perilous Times*, 277.

80 "We believe that anyone . . . enlistment is discouraged": Ibid.

81 "some get hurt . . . spill any blood": Wagner et al., *The Library of Congress World War II Companion*, 813.

83 "We have drawn a line . . . rather than let it happen": Hamm et al., *The Greenwood Library of American War Reporting: The Korean War*, 294.

83 "In the past week . . . you are advancing": Hamm et al., 271–272.

83–84 "The bedraggled soldiers . . . but a slaughter": Hamm et al., 274.

84–85 "Correspondents are not supposed . . . on the ground": Hamm et al., 296.

CHAPTER 5: CIVIL RIGHTS, VIETNAM, AND THE NEWS MEDIA

89 "police armed with shotguns . . . College Campus": David L. Hudson Jr., "Libel & Defamation," Freedom Forum Institute, September 13, 2002, www.freedomforuminstitute.org/2002/09/13/libel-defamation.

90 "[D]own in our part . . . the pressure": "Chapter 6: Newspapers and the Civil Rights Movement, 1954–1957," David R. Davies' Web Page, ocean.otr.usm.edu/~w304644/ch6.html.

90 "It is terribly difficult . . . local editors": Matthew Webster, "The Border Crossed Us," *Nonviolent Migration*, October 19, 2007, nonviolentmigration .wordpress.com/2007/10/19/the-border-crossed-us/.

91–92 "We consider this case . . . constitutional protection": *New York Times Co. v. Sullivan*, Legal Information Institute, Cornell Law School, www.law.cornell.edu /supremecourt/text/376/254.

92 "the fear of damage . . . Alabama courts": *New York Times Co. v. Sullivan*.

92 "actual malice" . . . "reckless disregard": *New York Times Co. v. Sullivan*.

93 "U.S. Calls . . . Racial Strife": *Detroit News*, Vol. 90, No. 255, May 4, 1963, www.pinterest.com/pin/176344141632417800/.

93 "About 100 negro . . . were attempted": Audie Cornish, "How The Civil Rights Movement Was Covered In Birmingham," June 18, 2013, www.npr.org /sections/codeswitch/2013/06/18/193128475/how-the-civil-rights-movement-was-covered-in-birmingham.

94 "The events in Birmingham . . . choose to ignore them": "The Birmingham Campaign," Black Culture Connection, PBS, www.pbs.org/black-culture /explore/civil-rights-movement-birmingham-campaign.

95 "Television will be a mighty . . . education and news": Charles L. Ponce de Leon, "Beginnings," *That's the Way It Is: A History of Television News in America*, Chicago: University of Chicago Press, 2015, website excerpt, www.press .uchicago.edu/books/excerpt/2015/De_Leon_Thats_Way_It_Is.html.

96 fewer than ten thousand television sets . . . two sets: "Number of Televisions in the US," *The Physics Factbook*, hypertextbook.com/facts/2007/Tamara Tamazashvili.shtml.

98 "If, when the chips . . . throughout the world": Richard Nixon, "Address to the Nation on the Situation in Southeast Asia—April 30, 1970," online transcript by Gerhard Peters and John T. Woolley, American Presidency Project, Richard Nixon Foundation, www.nixonfoundation.org/2017/09/address -nation-situation-southeast-asia-april-30-1970/.

98 419 accredited members of the press corps: Alan Rohn, "Media Role in the Vietnam War," *The Vietnam War*, March 2, 2014, thevietnamwar.info/media -role-vietnam-war.

99 "in which attacking . . . virtually inevitable": David Halberstam, "Vietnam

Defeat Shocks U.S. Aides," *New York Times*, January 7, 1963, *New York Times* Archives, www.nytimes.com/1963/01/07/archives/vietnam-defeat-shocks -us-aides-saigons-rejection-of-advice-blamed.html.

99–100 "We were right with the soldiers . . . got with the men": "Walter Cronkite: On Censorship," *Reporting America at War*, PBS, www.pbs.org/weta /reportingamericaatwar/reporters/cronkite/censorship.html.

100–101 "We had to file it . . . had been claimed": "Walter Cronkite."

101 "American Marines are . . . city is dead": Shafer, ed., *The Legacy*, 41.

102 "It seems now more certain . . . in a stalemate": Shafer, 142.

102 "they should have had censorship . . . prolonging the killing": "Walter Cronkite: On Censorship."

102 "Any war situation . . . there for history": "Walter Cronkite."

102 "Every American wants peace in Viet Nam.": "Richard Nixon for President 1968 Campaign Brochures, 'the Nixon stand,'" www.4president .org/brochures/1968/nixon1968brochure.htm.

103, 104 "Never forget . . . blackboard 100 times": "Presidents and the Press: Richard Nixon," ABC News, abcnews.go.com/Politics/photos/presidents- press-47795280/image-richard-nixon-47846492.

105 "the unauthorized possession . . . injury of the United States": "U.S. Code § 793: Gathering, Transmitting or Losing Defense Information," Legal Information Institute, Cornell Law School, www.law.cornell.edu/uscode /text/18/793.

107 "It is Jew thugs . . . in the city": Zac Farber, "Politics of the Past: When Min- nesota Tried to Stop the Presses," *Minnesota Lawyer*, January 18, 2017, minnlawyer.com/2017/01/18/politics-of-the-past-when-minnesota-tried-to -stop-the-presses.

107 "malicious . . . other periodical": Farber.

107 "tyrannical . . . oppressive": Farber.

107 "It is well understood . . . to be unrestrained": *Near v. Minnesota*, Legal Information Institute, Cornell Law School, 2018, www.law.cornell.edu /supremecourt/text/283/697.

108–109 "Only a free . . . trusted they would do": *New York Times Co. v. United States*, Legal Information Institute, Cornell Law School, www.law.cornell.edu /supremecourt/text/403/713.

CHAPTER 6: FREEDOM FOR THE STUDENT PRESS

112–113 "It can hardly be argued . . . rights of others": *Tinker v. Des Moines Independent Community School District*, Legal Information Institute, Cornell Law School, www.law.cornell.edu/supremecourt/text/393/503.

115–116 "A school must be able . . . legitimate pedagogical concerns": "Text of the Ruling in *Hazelwood School District v. Kuhlmeier*," *Education Week*, January 20, 1988, www.edweek.org/ew/articles/1988/01/20/07410060.h07.html.

116 "The young men and women . . . our constitution guarantees": *Hazelwood School District et al. v. Kuhlmeier et al.*, UMKC School of Law, law2.umkc.edu /faculty/projects/ftrials/firstamendment/hazelwood.html.

117 "I believe that freedom . . . our surroundings": Author email interview with Sienna E., May 2, 2019.

117 "The media occupies . . . those components": Author email interview with Kelly A., April 30, 2019.

117 "I don't believe that the free speech . . . especially crucial": Author email interview with Arthur K., April 11, 2019.

118 "I think there are definitely . . . serious topics forever": Author email interview with Sienna E., May 2, 2019.

118 "Nobody should ever be restricted . . . on a daily basis": Author email interview with Kelly A., April 30, 2019.

118–119 "in November 2018 . . . public forum": Author email follow-up interview with Kelly A., May 7, 2019.

120 "Earlier in this school year . . . big national issue right now": Author email follow-up interview with Arthur K., May 5, 2019.

120 "involved in the editorials . . . and misgendering": Author email follow-up interview with Alissandre C., May 10, 2019.

121 "We may not know it . . . world without any filters": Christina Barron, "On World Press Freedom Day, Student Shares Her Opinion on Why a Free Press Matters," *Washington Post*, May 2, 2017, www.washingtonpost.com/lifestyle

/kidspost/for-world-press-freedom-day-a-look-at-how-the-us-media-is-ranked
-globally/2017/05/02/a4fc568c-293c-11e7-a616-d7c8a68c1a66_story.html.

CHAPTER 7: NATIONAL SECURITY, 9/11, AND PRESS CENSORSHIP

125 "the press gave the American people . . . they ever had": Pete Williams, "View
from the Pentagon," *Washington Post*, March 17, 1991, www.washington
post.com/archive/opinions/1991/03/17/view-from-the-pentagon
/ef620cec-c4d9-40d1-93a8-f91db8468d3e.

125 "concerned 95 percent . . . not security": "Reporting America At War. The
Reporters." Christiane Amanpour, www.pbs.org/weta/reportingamericaatwar
/reporters/amanpour/poolsystem.html.

127 43 percent of Americans: Elisa Shearer, "Social Media Outpaces Print
Newspapers in the U.S. as a News Source," Pew Research Center, December
10, 2018, www.pewresearch.org/fact-tank/2018/12/10/social-media-
outpaces-print-newspapers-in-the-u-s-as-a-news-source.

129 "Act of War": Mark Abadi, "'America's Darkest Day': See Newspaper
Headlines from Around the World 24 Hours After 9/11," *Business Insider*,
September 10, 2019, www.businessinsider.com/september-11-911-
newspaper-headlines-2018-9.

129 "Terrorists Strike . . . 'Horrendous'": Abadi.

129 "U.S. Attacked": Abadi.

129 "a creeping horror": Abadi.

129 "Outrage": Abadi.

129 "America's Darkest Day": Abadi.

129 "It's War": Abadi.

130 "The face of terror . . . as much as I do": "'Islam Is Peace' Says President :
Remarks by the President at Islamic Center of Washington, D.C.," Office of
the Press Secretary, The White House, September 17, 2001, georgewbush
-whitehouse.archives.gov/news/releases/2001/09/20010917-11.html.

132 "The media have really flown . . . the war effort": David Shaw, "Media
Under Public Barrage over Content of War Coverage," *Los Angeles Times*,
November 18, 2001, www.latimes.com/archives/la-xpm-2001-nov-18-mn
-5607-story.html.

133 "Our intelligence officials . . . nerve agent": "Transcript of State of the Union, Part 8: Iraq," Inside Politics, CNN.com, January 29, 2003, www.cnn.com/2003/ALLPOLITICS/01/28/sotu.transcript.8/index.html.

133 "Iraq . . . biological weapons capability": Stephen Zunes, "The Case Against War: Ten Years Later," Institute for Policy Studies, September 11, 2012, ips-dc .org/the_case_against_war_ten_years_later.

133–134 "a scientist who claims . . . blocks of illegal weapons": Judith Miller, "Aftereffects: Prohibited Weapons; Illicit Arms Kept Till Eve of War; an Iraqi Scientist Is Said to Assert," *New York Times*, April 21, 2003, www.nytimes .com/2003/04/21/world/aftereffects-prohibited-weapons-illicit-arms-kept-till -eve-war-iraqi-scientist.html.

134 "Scientist Says Iraq Retained Illicit Weapons": James Moore, "That Awful Power: How Judy Miller Screwed Us All," *Huffington Post*, August 1, 2005, 2019, www.huffpost.com/entry/that-awful-power-how-judy_b_4986.

134 "Outlawed Arsenals . . . Before the War": Moore.

135 "It is not our job . . . and evasions": Shaw, "Media Under Public Barrage over Content of War Coverage", November 18, 2001, www.latimes.com/archives /la-xpm-2001-nov-18-mn-5607-story.html.

135 about six hundred journalists: Terence Smith, "Embedded Journalists in Iraq: War Stories," transcript, *PBS News Hour*, April 1, 2003, www.pbs.org /newshour/show/embedded-journalists-in-iraq-war-stories.

135–136 "But embedding comes . . . hardly a full picture": David Ignatius, "Embedded Journalism, in War & Politics," *Real Clear Politics*, May 2, 2010, www.realclearpolitics.com/articles/2010/05/02/embedded_journalism_in_war __politics.html.

138 "The charges . . . keep secret": Bart Jansen, "'Julian Assange Is No Journalist': Feds Charge WikiLeaks Founder for Revealing U.S. Government Secrets," *USA Today*, May 23, 2019, www.usatoday.com/story/news /politics/2019/05/23/wikileaks-founder-julian-assange-indicted-leaks -conspiracy-manning/1207119001.

138–139 "Any government use . . . in the public interest": "Reporters Committee Statement on Latest Assange Indictment," Reporters Committee for Freedom of the Press, May 23, 2019, www.rcfp.org/may-2019-rcfp-assange-statement.

139 eight people—were charged: Brittany Gibson, "All the President's Whis-

tleblowers," *The American Prospect*, October 18, 2019, prospect.org/justice /all-the-presidents-whistleblowers/.

139 On access to information: Reporters Committee for Freedom of the Press. January 23, 2012, www.rcfp.org/foia-panelists-say-obama-has-far-go-transparency/.

140 "Freedom of Information Improvement Act": Josh Gerstein, "Obama signs FOIA reform bill," *Politico*, June 30, 2016, www.politico.com/blogs/under-the -radar/2016/06/obama-signs-foia-reform-bill-225010.

140 Bill Clinton held fifteen . . . Donald Trump held one: Martha Joynt Kumar, "Six Presidents and Their Interchanges with Reporters from Inauguration Day to April 29th of the Second Year: 465 Days into the Administration," White House Transition Project, www.whitehousetransitionproject.org /wp-content/uploads/2018/05/Presidential_Interchanges_with_Reporters _FINAL_5-30-2018.pdf.

141 Trump tweeted 3,201 times: Steven Nelson, "Trump Triples Obama in Reporter Q&As, but Gives Half as Many Interviews," *Washington Examiner*, May 31, 2018, www.washingtonexaminer.com/news/white-house/trump -triples-obama-in-reporter-q-as-but-gives-half-as-many-interviews.

CHAPTER 8: FAKE NEWS, REAL LIES, AND THE PRESS

143 "They averaged four feet . . . and had wings": Kevin Young, "Moon Shot: Race, a Hoax, and the Birth of Fake News," *New Yorker*, October 21, 2017, www.newyorker.com/books/page-turner/moon-shot-race-a-hoax-and-the-birth -of-fake-news.

143 "by means of a telescope . . . a hundred yards": Young.

146 "the capacity to disseminate . . . a common conversation": Levi Boxell, Matthew Gentzkow, and Jesse M. Shapiro, "The Internet, Political Polarization, and the 2016 Election," Cato Institute, November 1, 2017, www.cato.org /publications /research-briefs-economic-policy/internet-political-polarization-2016-election.

147 "Nothing on this page is real": Eli Saslow, "'Nothing on This Page Is Real': How Lies Become Truth in Online America," *Washington Post*, November 17, 2018, www.washingtonpost.com/national/nothing-on-this-page-is-real -how-lies-become-truth-in-online-america/2018/11/17/edd44cc8-e85a -11e8-bbdb-72fdbf9d4fed_story.html.

147–148 "Any negative polls are fake news": Maya Rhodan, "President Trump

Defends Travel Ban: 'Any Negative Polls Are Fake News,'" *Time*, February 6, 2017, time.com/4660961/donald-trump-travel-ban-polls-fake-news.

148 "the FAKE NEWS media": William Cummings, "Trump Declares 'Fake News' Media 'the Enemy of the American People,'" *USA Today*, February 17, 2017, updated February 19, 2017, www.usatoday.com/story /news/politics/onpolitics/2017/02/17/trump-news-media-enemy-american -people/98065338.

148–149 "In 2017 . . . a beacon for repression": Tim Hains, "Full FOX News Interview: President Trump on Divided Congress, Mueller, Foreign Policy, Fake News, More," *Real Clear Politics*, November 18, 2018, www.realclearpolitics.com /video/2018/11/18/president_trump_on_divided_congress_mueller_foreign _policy_fake_news_more.html.

149 "Don't believe the . . . not what's happening": "Remarks by President Trump at the Veterans of Foreign Wars of the United States National Convention—Kansas City, MO," WhiteHouse.gov, July 24, 2018, www.whitehouse.gov/briefings-statements/remarks-president-trump-veterans -foreign-wars-united-states-national-convention-kansas-city-mo.

149 "Today, we were disappointed . . . have them there": Daniel Chaitin, "Veterans Group 'Disappointed' Some Members Booed Press During Trump Speech," *Washington Examiner*, July 24, 2018, www.washingtonexaminer.com /news/veterans-group-disappointed-some-members-booed-press-during -trump-speech.

150 "Like so many of my colleagues . . . U.S. war zones?": Martha Raddatz, "I Reported Along Soldiers in Foxholes. The President Can't Take That Away," *Washington Post*, July 24, 2018, www.washingtonpost.com /opinions/i-reported-alongside-soldiers-in-foxholes-the-president-cant-take -that-away/2018/07/24/0aa84746-8f8c-11e8-b769-e3fff17f0689_story.html.

151 "I just cannot state . . . Enemy of the People!": Dean Obeidallah, "When Trump Attacks the Media as the 'Enemy of the People,' People Like Robert Chain Believe Him," Think, NBCNews.com, September 2, 2018, www.nbcnews .com/think/opinion/trump-s-attacks-media-are-going-get-someone-killed -robert-ncna905541.

151 "The Fake News hates me . . . dangerous & sick": Harriet Sinclair, "Trump: Press Can Cause Wars and I'm 'Providing a Great Service' by Telling People

About It," *Newsweek*, August 5, 2018, www.newsweek.com/trump
-press-can-cause-wars-and-im-providing-great-service-telling-people-1057551.

152 "Any guy that can do . . . tough cookie": Greg Re, "Trump praises 'tough
cookie' Montana rep who 'body slammed' reporter last year, urges voters to
'never forget Benghazi,'" *Fox News*, October 18, 2018, www.foxnews.com
/politics/trump-hosts-rally-in-montana-to-campaign-against-longtime-bitter
-rival-jon-tester.

152 "Why do we work so hard . . . take away credentials?": Dara Lind,
"President Donald Trump Finally Admits That 'Fake news' Just Means
News He Doesn't Like," *Vox*, May 9, 2018, www.vox.com/policy-and
-politics/2018/5/9/17335306/trump-tweet-twitter-latest-fake-news-credentials.

152 "With all of the Fake News . . . Bad for country": Mark Joyella, "Sorry,
Mr. President, You Can't Challenge NBC's 'License' over 'Fake News,'" *Forbes*,
October 11, 2017, www.forbes.com/sites/markjoyella/2017/10/11/trump
-threatens-to-challenge-nbcs-license-over-fake-news/#7076541e6a12.

152 "Look at their license?": Makini Brice and David Shephardson, "Trump Hits
CNN and NBC, Urges 'Look at Their License': Tweet," Reuters.com,
September 4, 2018, www.reuters.com/article/us-usa-trump-media/trump
-hits-cnn-and-nbc-urges-look-at-their-license-tweet-idUSKCN1LK1Z1.

153 more than 250 journalists . . . including four women: Elana Beiser,
"Hundreds of Journalists Jailed Globally Becomes the New Normal,"
Committee to Protect Journalists, December 13, 2018, cpj.org/reports/2018
/12/journalists-jailed-imprisoned-turkey-china-egypt-saudi-arabia.php.

153 fifty-six journalists were killed: "56 Journalists Killed in 2018
/Motive Confirmed," CPJ Data, Committee to Protect Journalists,
cpj.org/data/killed/2018/?status=Killed&motiveConfirmed%5B%5D
=Confirmed&type%5B%5D=Journalist&start_year=2018
&end_year=2018&group_by=location.

153 "The tragedy reminds us . . . targeted by this attack": Meghan Keneally,
"9 Journalists Killed in Afghanistan: This Is 'A Reminder of the Extreme Dangers
to Media Workers,'" ABCNews.com, April 30, 2018, abcnews.go.com
/International/journalists-killed-afghanistan-reminder-extreme-dangers
-media-workers/story?id=54834057.

155 "liberal and conservative . . . join us": Editorial Board, "Journalists Are Not the Enemy," *Boston Globe*, August 16, 2018, p. 1, apps.bostonglobe .com/opinion/graphics/2018/08/freepress/p1=HP_special.

155 "'relentless assault . . . consequences'": Editorial Board.

155 "Lies are antithetical . . . more than two centuries": Editorial Board, 12.

155, 157 "We're at high school . . . lead better lives": "Editorial: The President Wants You to Think We're the Enemy. Here's What We Really Do," *Hartford Courant*, August 16, 2018, www.courant.com/opinion/editorials/hc-ed-enemy-of-the -american-people-20180810-story.html.

156 "devote reasonable attention . . . not necessarily equal": "Overview: The Rise of Talk Radio," *The Fire Next Time*, PBS Premiere: July 12, 2015, POV.org, archive.pov.org/thefirenexttime/overview-the-rise-of-talk-radio.

157 "During the tumultuous summer . . . prevent from happening": Charlie Smith, "The Ultimate Friend of the People," Columbian-Progress.com, August 14, 2018, www.columbianprogress.com/opinion-editorials/ultimate-friend -people-0#sthash.S5k7mqcU.dpbs.

157 "the attack potential dictators . . . want to say": Editorial Board, 13.

157 "We certainly don't . . . not free speech": "Remarks by President Trump at the Presidential Social Media Summit," WhiteHouse.gov, July 12, 2019, www.whitehouse.gov/briefings-statements/remarks-president-trump -presidential-social-media-summit.

157 "The Failing . . . of the People!": Ryan Saavedra, "Trump Levels CNN, New York Times While Issuing Warning to Mexico," *Daily Wire*, June 10, 2019, www. dailywire.com/news/trump-levels-cnn-new-york-times-while-issuing -ryan-saavedra.

159 "it's frankly disgusting . . . want to write": Andrew Prokop, "Trump: 'It's Frankly Disgusting the Press Is Able to Write Whatever They Want,'" *Vox*, October 11, 2017, www.vox.com/policy-and-politics/2017/10/11 /16460206/trump-press-disgusting.

159 "I do believe . . . core American principle": "Interview of Vice President Pence by Anna Palmer and Jake Sherman, 'Politico Playbook Live,'" WhiteHouse.gov, October 30, 2018, www.whitehouse.gov/briefings -statements/interview-vice-president-pence-anna-palmer-jake-sherman -politico-playbook-live.

159 "You're seen . . . as a beacon for repression": Tim Hains, "Full FOX News Interview: President Trump on Divided Congress, Mueller, Foreign Policy, Fake News, More," *Real Clear Politics*, November 18, 2018, www.realclearpolitics.com /video/2018/11/18/president_trump_on_divided_congress_mueller_foreign _policy_fake_news_more.html.

159 Myanmar official uses "fake news": David Nakamura, "House approves resolution calling persecution of Myanmar's Muslims a 'genocide' in contrast with Trump's silence," *Washington Post*, December 13, 2018, www. washingtonpost.com/politics/house-approves-resolution-calling-persecution -of-myanmar-muslims-a-genocide-in-contrast-with-trumps-silence/2018/12 /13/141c43ce-fef7-11e8-ad40-cdfd0e0dd65a_story.html.

CHAPTER 9: KEEPING THE PRESS SAFE FOR DEMOCRACY

162–163 "He made a series . . . 'zero' (no)": "President Trump Has Made More Than 10,000 False or Misleading Claims," The Fact Checker, *Washington Post*, August 2, 2019, www.washingtonpost.com/politics/2019/04/29/president -trump-has-made-more-than-false-or-misleading-claims.

163 "Fox Business host . . . for the [U.S.] government": Sean Higgins, "Fox's Neil Cavuto Says Trump 'Lying' on Tariff Math," *Washington Examiner*, May 14, 2019, www.washingtonexaminer.com/policy/economy/fox-business-neil -cavuto-says-trump-lying-on-tariff-math.

163–164 "Watching @FoxNews . . . who got them there": Matthew Rosza, "Donald Trump Says Watching Fox News 'Is Worse Than Watching Low Ratings Fake News CNN,'" July 8, 2019, www.salon.com/2019/07/08/donald-trump-says -watching-fox-news-is-worse-than-watching-low-ratings-fake-news-cnn.

167 "If there is any principle . . . thought that we hate": Lewis, *Freedom for the Thought That We Hate*, 37.

167 Reporters Without Borders rankings: "Index Details: Data of Press Freedom Ranking 2019," Reporters Without Borders, rsf.org/en/ranking_table.

167 Reporters Without Borders criteria: Reporters Without Borders, "Detailed Methodology," rsf.org/en/detailed-methodology.

167–168 "President Trump continued . . . and even polling stations": "RSF Index 2019: Institutional Attacks on the Press in the US and Canada," World Press Freedom Index 2019, Reporters Without Borders, rsf.org/en/rsf-index-2019 -institutional-attacks-press-us-and-canada.

SELECTED BIBLIOGRAPHY

*Indicates books suitable for young readers

Abernathy, Scott. *American Government: Stories of a Nation, Essential Edition.* Washington, D.C.: CQ, 2017.

Abrams, Floyd. *Speaking Freely: Trials of the First Amendment.* New York: Viking, 2005.

Cooke, John Byrne. *Reporting the War: Freedom of the Press from the American Revolution to the War on Terrorism.* New York: Palgrave Macmillan, 2007.

Epps, Garrett, ed. *Freedom of the Press: The First Amendment: Its Constitutional History and the Contemporary Debate.* Amherst, NY: Prometheus, 2008.

*Fireside, Harvey. *New York Times v. Sullivan: Affirming Freedom of the Press.* Springfield, NJ: Enslow, 1999.

*Fuller, Sarah Betsy. *Hazelwood v. Kuhlmeier: Censorship in School Newspapers.* Springfield, NJ: Enslow, 1998.

Hamm, Bradley, Donald L. Shaw, and Douglass K. Daniel. *The Greenwood Library of American War Reporting: World War II, the Asian Theater & the Korean War.* Vol. 6. Westport, CT: Greenwood, 2005.

International Encyclopedia of Communications. Vol. 3. Oxford: Oxford University Press and Philadelphia: Annenberg School of Communications, 1989.

*Levinson, Cynthia, and Sanford Levinson. *Fault Lines in the Constitution: The Framers, Their Fights, and the Flaws That Affect Us Today.* Atlanta: Peachtree, 2017.

Levy, Leonard W. *Emergence of a Free Press.* Chicago: Ivan R. Dee, 1985.

Lewis, Anthony. *Freedom for the Thought That We Hate: A Biography of the First Amendment*. New York: Basic Books, 2007.

LoMonte, Frank D., Adam Goldstein, and Michael Hiestand. *Law of the Student Press*. 4th ed. Arlington, VA: Student Press Law Center, 2013.

*Osborne, Linda Barrett. *Come On In, America: The United States in World War I*. New York: Abrams, 2017.

Powe, Lucas A., Jr. *The Fourth Estate and the Constitution: Freedom of the Press in America*. Berkeley: University of California Press, 1991.

Reynolds, Amy, and Debra Reddin van Tuyll. *The Greenwood Library of American War Reporting: The Civil War, North and South*. Vol. 3. Westport, CT: Greenwood, 2005.

*Rokutani, John. *Freedom of Speech, the Press, and Religion: The First Amendment*. New York: Enslow, 2018.

Shafer, D. Michael, ed. *The Legacy: The Vietnam War in the American Imagination*. Boston: Beacon, 1990.

*Sheinkin, Steve. *Most Dangerous: Daniel Ellsberg and the Secret History of the Vietnam War*. New York: Roaring Brook, 2015.

Shipler, David K. *Freedom of Speech: Mightier Than the Sword*. New York: Knopf, 2015.

Stone, Geoffrey R. *Perilous Times: Free Speech in Wartime*. New York: W. W. Norton, 2004.

*Sullivan, George. *Journalists at Risk: Reporting America's Wars*. Minneapolis: Twenty-First Century Books, 2006.

Wagner, Margaret, Linda Barrett Osborne, and Susan Reyburn. *The Library of Congress World War II Companion*. New York: Simon & Schuster, 2007.

Warburton, Nigel. *Free Speech: A Very Short Introduction*. Oxford: Oxford University Press, 2009.

IMAGE CREDITS

Unless otherwise indicated, all Library of Congress images are from the Prints and Photographs Division. The negative numbers to locate each image on the Library website are given.

Page 2: Library of Congress LC-USZ62-90742. **Page 5:** Library of Congress LC-USZ62-25244. **Page 6:** Library of Congress LC-DIG-ds-00123. **Page 8:** AP Photo/J. Scott Applewhite. **Page 10:** Library of Congress LC-USZ62-90299. **Page 12:** Courtesy National Park Service. **Page 13:** Courtesy National Park Service. **Page 16:** Library of Congress LC-USZ62-49739. **Page 18:** Library of Congress LC-USZ62-70245. **Page 20:** New York Public Library. **Page 23:** Eon Images. **Page 24:** Library of Congress LC-USZ62-21637. **Page 26:** Library of Congress LC-USZC4-5280. **Page 28:** Library of Congress LC-USZ62-43931. **Page 32:** Library of Congress LC-USZ62-1798. **Page 34:** Library of Congress LC-DIG-ppmsca-31832. **Page 36:** Library of Congress LC-DIG-ds-07444. **Page 39:** Library of Congress LC-DIG-ggbain-11433. **Page 41:** Library of Congress LC-DIG-cal-2a14550. **Page 44:** Library of Congress LC-DIG-ggbain-21591. **Page 46:** Library of Congress LC-DIG-ggbain-00336. **Page 48:** Library of Congress LC-USZ62-92298. **Page 52:** Library of Congress LC-DIG-pga-00295. **Page 55:** Library of Congress LC-DIG-pga-0035. **Page 57:** Library of Congress LC-USZ62-13961. **Page 59:** Library of Congress Rare Books and Special Collections. **Page 60:** Library of Congress LC-DIG-cwpb-01704. **Page 62:** Library of Congress LC-USZ62-68002. **Page 64:** Library of Congress LC-DIG-ppmsca-00180. **Page 65:** Alamy. **Page 66:** Library of Congress LC-USZ62-85573. **Page 68:** University of Chicago Library. **Page 71:** Library of Congress LC-USZ62-19866. **Page 75:** Library of Congress LC-USZ62-57002. **Page 76:** Library of Congress LC-DIG-hec-47251. **Page 77:** Library of Congress LC-DIG-hec-27208. **Page 79:** Library of Congress LC-DIG-

ACKNOWLEDGMENTS

I have had the good fortune to work on this, my fifth book with editor Howard Reeves. Howard is a master of knowledge and intuition about what goes into good nonfiction for kids. His guidance and support are invaluable. Many thanks to designers Erich Lazar and Heather Kelly for the creative and handsome way they have complemented the text with their work. I am also grateful to editorial assistants Sara Sproull and Emily Daluga for the seemingly effortless and gracious way they handle the continual flow of questions, changes, and requests that come with the making of a book.

Thanks also to managing editor Marie Oishi and production manager Kathy Lavisolo for deftly guiding *Guardians of Liberty* through the demanding process of going from manuscript to print. Copyeditor Rob Sternitzky did an excellent job of helping to ensure the accuracy and clarity of the book, as did proofreader Regina Castillo. Thanks to Tricia Kallett as well, for helping to ensure accuracy.

I appreciate the assistance in researching for text and finding images of Peter Tague of Georgetown University Law School; Rick Mastroianni, director of the Newseum Library; Gary Johnson of the Periodicals and Newspaper Division of the Library of Congress; Nathan King of the National Park Service; and Charles E. Brown of the St. Louis Mercantile Library. Thanks very much to Aimee Hess Nash and Susan Reyburn, once colleagues, now friends, for helping me obtain scans and for their continued support for my work. I also want to thank the student journalists who took the time to contribute their insights.

I am touched by the way friends rally around me when I write a book. Pam Zurer, Mary Glen Chitty, Ken Meter, Stella Richardson, Vincent Virga, and Peggy Wagner have especially provided sound advice and much needed encouragement for *Guardians*.

As always, I give special thanks to my husband, Bob, daughter, Catherine, son, Nick, and daughter-in-law, Mary Kate Hurley, for being there for me at every stage of the process. They have shared my passion and my discoveries and listened to all my thoughts on freedom of the press. Without them, writing would be much harder.

INDEX